Prais...
Negotiating the Sweet Spot

"Any relationship, be it personal, business, or otherwise, needs inter-actions that yield consistent win-win results if it is to succeed over time. Dr. Leigh Thompson has applied her expertise in compre-hensive research to take this 'why' we recognize and explain the 'what' behind it and the 'how' to achieve it. Translating this re-search to application, Dr. Thompson, the educator, uses her mas-tery of guiding students from theoretical knowledge to effective application by providing a toolkit of easy-to-use hacks and relatable anecdotes. *Negotiating the Sweet Spot* will certainly spend more time open on my desk than it will sitting on my shelf."

—STAN RUSSELL,
Executive Director of Alexion Pharmaceuticals

"Thompson's *Negotiating the Sweet Spot* provides valuable lessons for navigating conflict in personal and business life. Each of the stories and best practices in this book leads the reader on a deeper dive into how to resolve, finesse, learn, and thrive when seated at the negoti-ation table of life."

—LIN SHIU YI,
Owner of Technigroup Far East
and Owner and CEO Cell Viable

"Leigh Thompson has done it again. This time, she applies years of research and classroom experience to the negotiation process. Thompson distills the behavioral science into simple methods we can all use. *Negotiating the Sweet Spot* is a must-read for practicing attorneys and others who want to negotiate more successfully in all aspects of their lives."

—KAREN MCGAFFEY,
Partner and National Environment, Energy,
and Resources Practice Chair at Perkins Coie LLP

"Navigating conflict is a sore spot for many of us—both in and out of work. This book makes it possible to rise above compromise and create options better than any one person might imagine. Finally, we can see the skills involved and how to build them in easy, practical ways. Now the sweet spot is not only possible, but we have a set of tools to get there!"

—ALISON NIEDERKORN,
Executive Leadership Designer,
Facilitator, and Coach at Google

"In sales on a daily basis, I face the challenge of building trust, accelerating customer success, and maximizing deal sizes. The tools in this book are a breakthrough in the field of negotiations and have had an immediate impact on my bottom line and business relationships, and at the same time have added immense value for my clients to achieve a true win-win at the end of a deal cycle."

—DENNIS RAISCH,
Senior Enterprise Account Executive at Salesforce

"Thompson's evidence-based, tangible, and practical tools have guided me in countless professional negotiations to levels of success that I could not have ever imagined. In *Negotiating the Sweet Spot*, the revelation that the universe of negotiations is vastly larger than just the ones faced in a boardroom will broaden your appreciation, as it has mine, of how to maximize mutual benefit and build strength into not only your professional but personal relationships."

—KEVIN A. KELLIHER,
Director of Business Strategy
and Operations at Frontier BPM Inc.

THE ART OF LEAVING
NOTHING ON THE TABLE

Negotiating
the Sweet
Spot

Leigh Thompson

KELLOGG SCHOOL OF MANAGEMENT | NORTHWESTERN UNIVERSITY

HarperCollins
LEADERSHIP

AN IMPRINT OF HarperCollins

Published by HarperCollins Leadership, an imprint of HarperCollins Focus LLC.

Book design by Aubrey Khan, Neuwirth & Associates.

ISBN 978-1-4002-1744-1 (eBook)
ISBN 978-1-4002-1743-4 (HC)

Library of Congress Control Number: 2020934156

Printed in the United States of America

20 21 22 23 LSC 10 9 8 7 6 5 4 3 2 1

This book is lovingly dedicated to my students who have shared with me their triumphs, challenges, and defeats at all of life's negotiation tables. Their stories have shaped my research, teaching, and the pages of this book.

Contents

Contents

Chapter Six
Sweet Spot Hacks for the Workplace   95

Chapter Seven
Sweet Spot Hacks for Virtual Life   141

Contents

Chapter Eight
Putting It All Together

Preface

THE CONCEPT OF "WIN-WIN" HAS BEEN AROUND FOR DEC-
ades. It sounds good. Sounds fair. Sounds like good business.
Sounds good for relationships. Actually, it sounds like a no-
brainer! But does it work? Do people actually reach "win-win"
outcomes in business and in personal life?

Unfortunately, the answer is most often "no." My research
has revealed that people routinely fail to capture maximum
potential gains in their personal and workplace negotiations.
For example, my simulation studies show that, on average,
talented managers leave about 20 percent of potential mutual gains untapped. That's akin to taking 20 percent of the
value of every business deal and dumping it into the trash. So,
in a typical $100,000 business deal, about $20,000 goes down
the drain.

My next question to the managers in my studies is about how often they negotiate. The most typical response is once-a-week or once-per-month. If we figure that in, we are now up to $200,000 a year in waste, or even more! And if we think about ten years of a career, a conservative estimate of the lost value associated with failure to reach win-win is about $2 million! Now, if you are a leader or manager and have, say, ten direct reports, we are now approaching $20 million of lost value when you include their failures to achieve win-wins! You can see where this is going. What may seem like a drop in the bucket is actually an ocean of losses!

We can calculate the same lost value when partners, friends, or family members consistently fail to satisfy one another's needs and end up disappointing themselves and hurting people they care about. Indeed, when it comes to our personal relationships, the stakes involved with maximizing the value of any kind of interaction are often much higher than in our professional lives. When we leave value on the table, the relationship can sour and, sometimes, dissolve altogether.

Learning how to get to that maximum value can mean the difference between successful and failed relationships, along with the ability or inability to actually enjoy our leisure time or balance our work and personal lives. Remember: Many people are conflict-avoidant when it comes to their personal relationships; unwilling to rock the boat, they keep the peace, often by second-guessing what their partners and loved ones want. In the meantime, the other partner is doing the exact same thing, resulting in suboptimal outcomes on multiple di-

mensions. The good news is that you don't have to be a licensed clinician to learn the strategies in this book and use
them to maximize the value of your relationships—something
I call finding the "sweet spot."

Traditionally, "win-win" negotiation has focused nearly exclusively on money and other economic resources, like services, products, market share, and financial returns. In this
book, the term "sweet spot" expands the scope to reflect all the
things that people care about in business and life, *which are not
always measured in dollars*. Thus, the sweet spot refers to money
as well as to intangible but infinitely valuable non-financial
resources. When people find the sweet spot, they maximize
value however they may define it: happiness, peace of mind,
contentment, satisfaction, relationship stability, and trust in
their personal relationships and business dealings. So, let's set
aside "win-lose" framing and instead focus on the sweet spot.

In this book I refer to situations in which people fail to
maximize the value in their business and personal relationships as "missing the sweet spot." Conversely, when they leverage their interests, needs, and desires in a way that creates
value for themselves and their business partners, spouses, and
friends, they are finding the sweet spot.

So, what's the problem? As we shall see, it's astounding
how often people miss sweet spot deals, including those right
in front of their faces. Why does this happen? It's not for lack
of trying. It's not because people's hearts and heads are in the
wrong place. It's because the sweet spot is *elusive*. Many people
fall into "traps" that pull them away from the sweet spot and

toward a sour-lemon outcome! Indeed, most of us have been taught to avoid conflict, divide things down the middle, or, in some cases, pound our fists on the table to get what we want. None of these tactics is effective in personal or business life.

Finding the sweet spot is a *skill*; like any skill, it takes practice. Most of us have not been taught this capability. Indeed, expecting people to find sweet spots without any training, practice, feedback, or experience is like shoving them onto a tennis court for the first time, with no coaching or instruction, and expecting them to just "pick it up."

Fortunately, there are surefire methods to get out of the quagmire and create meaningful, lasting value in relationships and business. Until now, these methods have been developed primarily for and offered to business students and executives in advanced management courses. I've devoted my career to studying how managers and executives negotiate; my resulting research has yielded a set of powerful techniques that can be used not only in the boardroom and conference room, but across the kitchen table. Prior to studying business negotiations, I earned a master's degree in Counseling Psychology. My experience in the counseling clinic gave me deep appreciation for how poor conflict resolution prevents people from reaching their own sweet spot outcomes with partners, spouses, children, and parents.

Here, I translate these surefire, research-backed best practices into life tools to use in daily negotiations and conflict situations. These tools can be useful in our personal relationships, at the workplace, and in virtual life. I call these tools "hacks" because they work well but don't require a lot of financial investment, training, or time. You don't have to be a CEO, senior VP, or regional brand manager to learn how to find the sweet spot in life's negotiations. You just have to be open to learning.

During the time I was writing this book, the world was shaken by the COVID-19 pandemic, the rapid spread of illness associated with the novel coronavirus discovered in late 2019. Literally overnight, the healthcare crisis and widespread stay-at-home orders led to the most radical restructuring of interactions and expectations most organizations and people had ever faced, catapulting personal, work, and community life into disarray. Businesses, communities, couples, and families underwent profound upheaval that affected personal relationships, the workplace, and virtual communication.

One of the most profound changes associated with the pandemic was the transition from the ease and comfort of face-to-face business meetings and interactions to virtual teams and work, including formal and informal negotiations. There was no memo. No training plan. No "onboarding" to the new reality. It just happened, and everyone had to adapt. That meant people had to quickly rethink and reengineer their personal and professional relationships and interactions while gaining or sharpening virtual collaboration skills. These dramatic events have profound implications for the ideas and tools in this book.

In the wake of a global "new normal," it is important not to blindly assume that the skills that worked in the conference room transfer seamlessly to a conference *call*—or that what's effective in person will continue to serve you well on-screen. Many families and couples had to "re-negotiate" their work and family life as they literally brought their workplace into their living rooms. Whether it is negotiating who gets the home office and who is stuck in a closet or how best to home-school children, the ability to look for a "sweet spot" amid the loss of relationships, jobs, and people in our lives has never been so important.

As people rebuild their lives, businesses, families, and communities, the ideas and tools you'll learn here should prove valuable. For example, chapter 7, "Sweet Spot Hacks for Virtual Life," offers key hacks and tips for getting the most out of virtual interactions, which represented a rising share of work and home life even before the COVID crisis. Overall, I present a full set of strategies for dealing with conflict in personal, business, and virtual life, whether associated with times of great change and stress or with life and business as usual. I'm confident what you gain will help you to find the sweet spot in the new lives that each of us is rebuilding post-COVID and well beyond. In general, I'm excited to teach you the sweet spot–finding skills I've learned over decades, so you can reap their many rewards. Finding the sweet spot not only feels good, but it preserves and enhances relationships, ensuring their long-term success, whether in personal, business, or virtual life.

Negotiating *the* Sweet Spot

CHAPTER ONE

What Is the Sweet Spot?

RECENTLY I WAS PART OF A DEVELOPMENT TEAM WITH several colleagues, designing a new online multi-course specialization. This was a mammoth project, and each of us faculty members working on it had our own idiosyncratic needs and predilections. I was admittedly one of the more "idiosyncratic" players, determined to do things my way. During a kick-off planning meeting, five of us sat around the table and did our best to balance speaking our minds with attempting to be collegial. We had to make several key decisions: the sequencing of the courses (i.e., who would teach first, second, etc.); the creation of a final project encompassing all material across the courses; the filming schedule; and other issues. I had strong feelings about all of these issues. I wanted my course to be first in the sequence (to accommodate my travel schedule),

I wanted to be filmed in the afternoons (knowing I would need a miracle hair and make-up session beforehand!), and I wanted as little to do with the final project as possible. However, I did not want to come in like a tiger, given that none of us had previous working relationships and appearing demanding would create and escalate tension in the group.

Then, something interesting happened just a few minutes into our first meeting. The project director—a high-level staff member—presented what she described as a "fair and reasonable" schedule on a pre-made PowerPoint. I wasn't pleased by what I saw on the screen: My course was scheduled second to last, I had to take the first crack at writing the final project, and the filming schedule was all over the map. Ugh. I glanced around and others seemed to be in silent agreement with her proposal.

After about forty-five minutes of indirect conversation, the meeting was adjourned. "Well, dealing with other faculty members is never easy," I consoled myself as I stood to leave. But as I walked out, another group member said, "I actually think it would make sense to have your course come first in the sequence." I said, "Really? Would you be okay with that?" Definitely, she said, because she had not yet written her content and needed a few more weeks to prepare. She added that my content would lay the groundwork well for the other courses. Seeing an opportunity, we quickly pulled the other three faculty members back into the room for an impromptu conversation. It turned out one of them wanted to write the final project because they were working on a large new business case; another wanted to film only in the morning due to afternoon childcare commitments. On the back of the Power-Point printouts, we sketched out a plan that was nothing like the "fair and reasonable" default, but that we all agreed was better. Within forty-five minutes, we'd found the sweet spot!

Looking back, I realized that I'd experienced a "near miss." My colleagues and I had almost gone down a path that would have resulted in wasted time, energy, sacrifice, and expense, not to mention simmering tension and resentment—all because we were convinced that other people held polar-opposite views, or at least didn't agree with us. Wanting to avoid stress, be good colleagues, and preserve our reputations, we'd silenced our objections and offered concessions. Luckily, we second-guessed ourselves and ultimately found the sweet spot, but may well not have! Think about how many times in life people settle for a less-than-optimal arrangement, including near misses.

People do this so much that there's even a name for it. Nobel Laureate Herb Simon coined the term "satisficing" to refer to situations in which people settle for less-than-optimal outcomes.[1]

Satisficing is the opposite of optimizing. When we satisfice, we settle, capitulate, throw in the proverbial towel. Conversely, when we optimize, we leverage all the potential in the relationship in a mutually rewarding fashion. So why do people satisfice instead of optimize? According to Simon, people are too lazy and miserly with their time to bother to think, research, and optimize. As "cognitive misers," Simon argues, people try to minimize energy expenditure and look for shortcuts.

Now hold on a minute. As a business school professor who teaches negotiation courses, I am surrounded by people who are anything but lazy! In fact, they are adamant about upping their game, and willing to devote significant time and energy into improving their skills in every element of business. There must be something else going on. In my research on negotiation, I've observed and measured three "traps" that effectively prevent people from finding the sweet spot.

The "Show Me the Money" Trap

Let's face it: Win-win in business negotiations usually involves money and other economically tangible resources that can be measured on some universal scale of utility. Because negotiation is typically equated with money, people believe they must choose between being self-interested (i.e., cutthroat) or a team player (i.e., taking one for the team). This false dichotomy results in two suboptimal strategies: people are either too aggressive or too capitulating. The truth is, most business managers care about money *and* relationships. Indeed, Pruitt and Rubin's Dual-Concern model argues that to the extent that negotiators can focus on *both* their own interests and those of the other party, they can find sweet spot deals.[2]

Now here's the rub: Most people believe that *other people* are self-interested. And this often sets businesspeople on a combative course. In short, we don't see others the way we see ourselves. For example, a large study of attorneys revealed that most are intrinsically motivated to do what they do; they're drawn to their profession because they want to make a positive difference. However, these same attorneys believe that their colleagues are strictly motivated by economic rewards (i.e., in it for the money).[3] Thus people are guilty of a double-standard: They believe others are motivated strictly by financial gain, but they themselves are uniquely focused on intrinsic values such as doing good for the world.

Similarly, a detailed study of competitive versus cooperative personality types found that competitors view the world as uniformly competitive but cooperators see the world as much more complex.[4] What does this all add up to? Because we see others as uniformly more self-interested than we are, we often go on the defensive when it comes to conflict, bracing ourselves for what seems to be a clash of interests. And in doing so, we confirm the other party's views about us—namely, they continue to see us as self-interested, and they act accordingly.

Moreover, making more money does not always make people feel more successful or satisfied. How do we know this? In one research investigation, I watched people negotiate and afterward asked them how "successful" they felt. People who had focused solely on their highest financial goals and aspirations felt *less* successful than people who had focused on their minimum goals.[5]

The study that really brought the seeming disconnect between money and relationships home for me was one that I did with my colleagues Rod Kramer and Kathleen McGinn.[6] We observed people negotiating and explored how people felt when their opponent appeared happy versus disappointed. We found that people felt *less* successful when they thought their opponent was happy and felt *more* successful when they thought their opponent was disappointed, because the latter suggested the person in question was "winning" the negotiation. In other words, most people reported thinking, "If the other party appeared happy and satisfied, then I must not have done that well!" However, the feeling of success was bittersweet because the people who felt successful also regarded themselves as less honorable in the negotiations. Thus, doing well financially was often experienced with ambivalence when the other party was dissatisfied.

The key point is that people care about money *and* relationships. So the quality of negotiation cannot be measured just in economic terms. The challenge is that most people don't know how to maximize both—so they choose one to max out or capitulate on both.

The breakthrough research of MIT business professor Jared Curhan on "subjective value" sheds important light on how most people really feel about their negotiations. Curhan and his colleagues developed an instrument known as the subjective value inventory (SVI) to assess four concerns that most negotiators bring to any negotiation table—whether it be the boardroom or the kitchen variety:[7]

- Feelings about instrumental outcomes (a.k.a., economics)
- Feelings about themselves
- Feelings about the process
- Feelings about the relationship with the other party

To prove his point—namely, that people care about more than just money and economics—Curhan looked at the values that people held most dear in their life negotiations, studying carefully the elements that students, community members, and practitioners believe to be of highest importance. He even examined the satisfaction of arguably the most economically-minded group of people he could find: full-time MBA students negotiating employment packages. This would seem to be a situation ripe for cutthroat economics! Imagine that you have just spent over $200,000 paying for a degree, taking tough classes, and losing two years of income, then being in a competitive job market with several hundred similarly accomplished friends and colleagues. Wouldn't you want to maximize your economic outcome?

But Curhan made a startling discovery. MBA students care about *all four* of the factors above as related to their future employment—and to the extent that they feel good about themselves, the process, and their relational and instrumental outcomes in the position they accept, they are *less* inclined to seek a different job the following year!

The "Even-Steven" Trap

The "Even-Steven" trap is the (usually) faulty belief that the best outcome in a conflict or negotiation situation divides scarce resources down the middle. Indeed, most people believe that the division of resources between people should always be equal or equitable. There's a reason we have so many strategies based on the "Even-Steven" principle: "split-the-difference"; "one divides, other chooses"; "let's-go-halfsies"; "meet you halfway"; "give a little, get a little"; and many others.

As part of my research, I ask businesspeople and nonprofessionals about ways to resolve conflicts and settle disputes. Hands down, the most common prescription I get is to *compromise*. "Give and take." And by the way, if I hear one more businessperson say, "I took one for the team," I'm going to scream!

As tempting as it may be to divide resources (like money) evenly, this is not actually what "win-win" means. Win-win is not about *dividing* the pie or the money or the value; rather, it's about *capturing all* the value.

My teaching and speaking has shown that the best way to illustrate the "Even Steven" trap is by telling my favorite story, one attributed to the wise teaching of behavioral scientist Mary Parker Follet.[8] Most recently, I shared this story with the ex-CEO of a large healthcare organization. He said, "Now that makes total and complete sense! It explains not only why people who work in the same organization should find the sweet spot, it also explains why you should find the sweet spot even when you are dealing with customers and suppliers."

Okay, back to the story. Picture two sisters sitting at a table with an orange between them. The sisters love each other, but they *both* want the orange. To complicate matters, there's some difficult family history, with a consistent pattern of competition between the sisters. "I'm not going to back down," one sister says. "Today, this orange is mine!" To that the other sister snaps, "No way! You got your way last time. It's my turn!" And the conflict escalates. Ultimately, they realize that preserving their long-term relationship is more important than the orange. So they agree to cut the orange exactly in half, using precise scientific measurement—"Even Steven."

After the dividing, one sister takes her half, squeezes out the juice, and tosses away the empty rind. Meanwhile, the other sister carefully zests her half of the orange peel (to make her favorite scone recipe) and throws the juice away. After the garbage truck comes and goes, understanding what happened, the sisters are aghast: "You mean, this whole time you only wanted the peel and I only wanted the juice, and now it's too late for us both to fully get what we wanted?"

So what happened to the sisters? They missed the sweet spot! They sliced the orange in half, falling into the "Even Steven" trap! They satisficed but failed to optimize. When we satisfice, we settle, capitulate, and compromise. When we optimize, we leverage, integrate, and expand the value. Even though the sisters cared about each other, they failed to maximize value.

Given how valuable that story has been for me, you can imagine my excitement when I encountered a real-world busi-

9

ness example of dividing the orange. In this case, it involved the Kellogg's cereal company (makers of Corn Flakes, Rice Krispies, and many others) and the Seven Brothers Brewery in Manchester, England. Keith McAvoy, the brewery's chief strategist and one of the seven brothers in its name, has spent his whole working life in the beer industry. When Keith learned that the local Kellogg's cereal factory generated more than 5,000 tons of wasted cereal (falling short of quality-control standards), he started to experiment with beer recipes. His experiment led to a partnership with Kellogg's and the production of *Toast Ale* and *Throw Away I.P.A.*—smooth, mellow beers made from corn flakes. So the brewery was able to use Kellogg's waste, but what's in it for the cereal maker? A 12.5 percent reduction in food waste for their UK facilities! So it's a win-win agreement for beer-drinkers and cereal-eaters alike.[9]

Here's my question to you, then: How often have you cut the orange in half, or thrown it across a room, or watched the garbage truck come and go? If you are like most of my managers and executives, you fail to optimize about 80 percent of the time. Specifically, what I typically find is that only 15 to 20 percent of managers *fully* leverage all the potential gains in their negotiations (a.k.a. "optimize")—meaning that 80 to 85 percent of people miss the sweet spot all together (a.k.a. "satisfice"). When I measure exactly how much value is left untapped, it typically amounts to about 20 to 25 percent! Unfortunately, most of the time people are unaware that they did not find the sweet spot!

The "Win-Win" Mirage

During any given week, I teach more than fifty managers and executives about negotiation, through role-play negotiation exercises. I routinely ask them to evaluate their outcomes prior to showing them a deep-dive analysis of their performance. About 99 percent of them strongly believe that their outcomes are, in fact, "win-win." When I ask them why, they say, "We reached an agreement and we're both happy." Then I give them the bad news: Their hard-fought negotiated outcomes are actually not win-win, meaning they left significant value on the table.

It's a seemingly universal problem, something I see routinely. Managers in every industry are under increasing pressure to make economic gains and negotiate good business deals with their suppliers, customers, clients, and stakeholders. Most of them are able to reach profitable business deals and most of them regard their outcomes to be "win-win." However, just like the sisters, they merely satisfice—they fail to optimize. As noted earlier, my research studies reveal that less than 20 percent of people find the "sweet spot"—the readily available solution that would be indisputably better for both parties. Why is this?

The key reason people fail to reach win-win is that *they don't see compromise solutions as failures.* If they did, they would be much more likely to abandon their current behaviors and adopt new ones. Thus suboptimal behavior (i.e., satisficing) is self-reinforcing. We think to ourselves, "I must be doing something right, because I reached a deal and made some profit." Bottom line: We don't know what we don't know. This is the "win-win mirage," the third trap that prevents people from finding the sweet spot.

The numbers can be dismal. In one research study that contained a hard-to-find win-win solution, I found that fewer than 4 percent of managers found the sweet spot (i.e., nearly everyone failed to maximize value) when put to the test.[10] Just like the sisters, even the most highly motivated negotiators don't recognize the opportunity.

I then started to wonder whether people might be so far down the rabbit hole that they would not even know when they were in 100 percent complete agreement with another person. So, in my doctoral dissertation, I included a simulation in which people had *identical* preferences—meaning they wanted the exact same thing! Specifically, it was a car negotiation in which the buyer and seller had obviously opposing interests when it came to price, financing terms, etc., but they actually were in complete alignment on the color—the dealer wanted to sell a certain color and the customer preferred that color as well. I called this alignment a "compatible" interest. My question was whether people would realize when they were in complete alignment with the other person. It almost seemed too silly a question to ask.

It wasn't. To my shock and amazement, I found that 50 percent of the time people believed that the other party had opposing interests even for a completely compatible one! I called this the "incompatibility effect."[11] This meant that people failed to realize when they were on the same page with another person—kind of like what happened in my development team with my fellow faculty members. Moreover, they immediately capitulated to the other person—i.e., made an unnecessary sacrifice. When they missed the sweet spot—that was right in front of them, in this case—I called it a *lose-lose* outcome: neither party got what they wanted!

To find out how widespread this "lose-lose" effect was, I did a large-scale study with Dennis Hrebec, my colleague at the University of Washington.[12] In addition to examining how often people failed to reach, much less even recognize, win-win outcomes, we looked at hundreds of published and unpublished studies and databases related to negotiation. These studies were analogous to the sisters-and-orange situation in that there was a non-obvious "sweet spot" solution that often eluded well-intentioned, highly motivated players. In our analysis of more than five thousand people, we discovered that negotiators failed to realize when they were in complete agreement with the other party about 50 percent of the time, and fell prey to the lose-lose effect about 20 percent of the time. In other words, even when people were in 100 percent agreement with each other, they didn't realize it nearly half the time!

This reality, when pointed out to negotiators, leads to what I've come to call the "Negotiation V8 moment," named after the old commercials for V8 vegetable juice, where people realize they should've had the healthy beverage instead of something else: "I should've had a V8!" In negotiation, it's something like, "I can't believe I didn't see that!" For example, I was once working with the attorneys in a large professional services firm. After completing a negotiation simulation, in which parties could land upon a true "sweet spot" agreement if they were able to identify their points of compatible alignment, only 15 percent actually discovered these mutual interests. The others falsely assumed that the counterparty had opposing interests, and thus failed to reach sweet spot deals. When I showed them the results, many of them had a "Negotiation V8" moment!

So why do people miss compatible issues and fail to identify even obvious sweet spot arrangements? A key reason is that most of the time, people assume that others have directly opposing goals; they hold a "fixed-pie" perception and believe that splitting the difference is the best they can do. However, splitting the difference is a *win-win mirage*, as discussed earlier, meaning that while it appears to be a way of embracing both parties' interests, it actually doesn't leverage the true interests of the parties.

In this book, I refer to arrangements that capture all the potential value in a relationship as the sweet spot because there often exists a near-optimal, highly satisfying, relationship-preserving solution for personal and business problems. The sweet spot is the solution that maximizes the value—both economic *and* relational—for everyone concerned.

CHAPTER TWO

Measuring the Sweet Spot

FOR ME, FINDING THE SWEET SPOT WAS LIKE SEARCHING for Bigfoot—it's elusive, but I was determined to locate and document it. As a behavioral scientist, I've spent the better part of my life tracking and measuring the sweet spot. As it turns out, the fields of economics, management science, and social psychology are largely in agreement on the sweet spot idea—even though they use different terminology.

In economics and game theory, the closest cousin to the sweet spot concept is what is known as the *Nash equilibrium*, based on the pioneering work of John Nash.[1] If you have not read his seminal papers, I find it useful (and fun!) to think about how the popular movie *A Beautiful Mind* portrays his thinking.[2] In one of my favorite scenes, John Nash (played by Russell Crowe) is seated in a crowded bar with friends as a group of attractive women enter. It is at that moment that Nash allegedly starts formulating his theory—ultimately known as the Nash equilibrium.

Setting aside any of Nash's predatory motivations with regard to dating, the idea is this: If all of the men attempt to attract the most desirable female, they end up blocking one another, resulting in a suboptimal outcome (that is, a lose-lose for all). Nash explains, further, that the other women do not want to be considered "second fiddle" and will surely rebuff them if they see the men become interested only after the most attractive woman rejected them. So, Nash proposes that they all resist attempting to pursue the most attractive woman, and each pursue another woman in the group, such that they all "win." At this point, Nash dashes out of the bar to go write his Nobel Prize–winning paper!

Italian economist Vilfredo Pareto made a simple and powerful related proposition: People should never settle for any outcome that both of them regard as less desirable than some other feasible outcome.[3] Well, in the last chapter, the sisters who split the orange did! And in my own situation with my colleagues on the course-development team (again in the previous chapter), we almost did! So, the *Pareto efficient frontier* is the set of possible outcomes (settlements) that leaves no portion of the total amount of resources unallocated.[4] Let's start with an economics-based explanation. Any option that is *not* on the Pareto frontier is worse for *everyone* than an option that *is* on the Pareto frontier. For example, suppose that a couple planning a vacation both prefer the mountains over the beach; if they end up at the beach, this is not on the Pareto frontier because they both prefer the mountains! Options that are not on the Pareto frontier are dominated by other viable solutions (just like a mountain vacation dominates a beach getaway for the couple in our example). Settlements that are dominated violate a fundamental principle of economics, the utility principle of maximization. The resolution of any negotiation should be an option from the Pareto efficient frontier because any other option unnecessarily requires more concessions on the part of one or both negotiators.

Good heavens, what does this all mean? I find that a useful way of thinking about Pareto optimization is to imagine that in every negotiation—whether it involves vacation plans, collaborative teamwork, a dinner date, or even a business deal, there are hundreds, thousands, and in some cases, millions of diamonds on a table. The diamonds are yours to keep, with just one condition: You and the other party (e.g., colleague, spouse, friend, partner, or business partner) must agree on how to divide them. Obviously, you want to get as many diamonds as you can, but so does the other party. To make things even more complicated, you don't know how many diamonds there are because a big blanket is covering them. Now, imagine you both leave half or one-third or some other amount of diamonds on the table, *without realizing it*. Then a sinkhole suddenly opens up under the table, and the diamonds are lost forever. This scenario is equivalent to failing to reach a Pareto-optimal agreement.

Most of us would never imagine allowing such an unfortunate event to happen. However, in many negotiation situations, people do just that—they leave diamonds on the table or money to burn, and trust is broken.

But it is possible to find the sweet spot. Consider how "Donna," the CEO of a professional services company, was able to find the diamonds in a sensitive human resources (HR) situation. Specifically, Donna was having trouble with "Callie," one of her managing directors in the East Coast office. To be sure, Callie was a fantastic director and a great resource for the client services team. But Callie wasn't very "available" to her colleagues and her clients. More to the point, Callie's calendar was blocked out every day between 3:00 p.m. and 5:00 p.m. One client bemoaned that they hadn't been able to schedule a thirty-minute phone call with Callie for over two months!

This lack of accessibility had a very negative effect on Callie's clients and colleagues alike. To further complicate matters, the organization was a ROWE environment (Results Only Work Environment), so employees did not feel compelled to be physically present, nor were they expected to be. In fact, it was rare for all team members to be physically co-present at a given time, with many involved in client projects at remote locations or working from home. However, Callie's calendar made her an outlier even in this environment. Understandably, Brenda, Callie's administrative assistant, grew increasingly frustrated trying to work with her managing director's mysterious calendar, and even felt demeaned by the task. With tensions rising, Donna thought her only option might be to ask Callie to leave, or perhaps to work part-time.

However, Donna ultimately decided to find out if there were some parts of the figurative orange that she didn't know about. During a meeting with Callie and Brenda, it became clear to Donna that there were at least three parts of the orange: training sessions, client coaching, and calendar scheduling. Even more enlightening, Callie and Brenda had very different preferences for those three issues. Brenda wanted to support and assist in client training sessions—something that Callie strongly preferred not to do. Conversely, Callie wanted to focus on coaching. And she wanted to manage her own calendar. So, Donna suggested that Brenda focus exclusively on training—no more calendar management—and that Callie focus only on coaching, and manage her own calendar. Callie and Brenda were completely over the moon! They had gotten their most preferred parts of the orange. Clients were also thrilled because they had easy, direct access to Brenda. And no one had to get fired or go part-time. Donna later reflected that the suboptimal, Pareto-inefficient situation had continued for over a year before they were able to find the sweet spot!

According to most economists, mathematicians, and game theorists, people should always reach the Pareto-optimal frontier. To do anything less, well, would be *irrational* and suboptimal. However, are people actually rational? This is where the work of behavioral scientists is very useful.

As a young doctoral student, I started to examine the question of whether people actually reach Pareto-optimal (sweet spot) deals. I researched, adopted, modified, and created scenarios that essentially modeled the sisters-and-orange situation, meaning that they contained sweet spot solutions—just like in the case of Callie and Brenda. During one early pilot test, I obtained access to a high-level executive group. I assigned them roles in a business situation and found that *nearly all* of them missed the sweet spot: They quickly divided the scarce resources down the middle—"Even Steven." A few particularly cutthroat managers failed to reach deals at all! When I showed them the sweet spot later, they were shocked but intrigued.

Wondering if I'd just gotten unusual results, I did the study again. Same outcome. Next, I tried several things that might help, such as giving them more time to prepare or more time to negotiate. Still, they consistently missed the sweet spot, quickly compromising in most cases. I even offered attractive monetary incentives for finding the sweet spot. No luck. When I consulted with colleagues at other universities, they reported similar results.

The sweet spot, it appeared, was universally elusive. So it was important to understand why, as we'll discuss next.

CHAPTER THREE

Why Do We Miss the Sweet Spot?

I took one for the team.   —*Business executive*

AS YOUNG PHD STUDENT, I WAS CURIOUS AS TO WHY PEO-ple so often fail to optimize in business and personal situations—and miss the sweet spot that seems obvious in hindsight. Now the truth is, at the time I was doing my dissertation research on a somewhat esoteric concept. Okay, it was downright boring and unimportant. *Good heavens*, I thought, *I'm in a sour spot myself!* So, I took a big professional risk. I completely switched dissertation topics, setting me back months. But I was committed to my quest to find out why people so often fail to reach win-win outcomes.

My next mission: I needed some way to measure this phenomenon that I was convinced was clouding negotiators' thinking. So, I started measuring something called the "fixed-pie perception." According to Bazerman and Neale, the fixed-pie perception is the belief held by many people that whatever they want in an interpersonal situation, the other party has completely opposing preferences.[1] If we put this in the context of the sisters-and-orange situation, the fixed-pie perception would be the strongly held (yet faulty) assumption by one sister that the other sister also wants the juice or rind—when in fact, that is not (always) true. I look back on my situation with my colleagues on the course-development team some time ago and realize that I had indeed fallen prey to the fixed-pie perception. Namely, I had falsely assumed that my colleagues would be solidly opposed to my preferences for filming, project-writing, and course sequencing.

Most negotiators, too, view negotiation as a competition: They assume that their interests are incompatible, in line with the fixed-pie perception.[2] I created an assessment tool to measure whether people held the fixed-pie perception. I used multiple methods to assess the magnitude of the (faulty) fixed-pie perception, including quizzes, questionnaires, and interviews with people in negotiation simulations. In one of my investigations, I measured negotiators' perceptions of the counterparty's interests immediately before, during, and following a negotiation.[3] The majority (68 percent) viewed the other's interests as completely opposed to their own, reflecting the fixed-pie perception! However, in fact, negotiators actually shared some interests that could be profitably traded off and, in some cases, were completely compatible.

Unfortunately, banishing the fixed-pie perception is difficult. It is not sufficient, for example, to warn negotiators of its existence.[4] Further, it's not enough for negotiators to have negotiation experience.[5] It is not even enough for negotiators to receive feedback about the counterparties' interests—the very thing they're making assumptions about![6] Moreover, lack of time and effort do not explain lose-lose outcomes and the fixed-pie perception. In fact, negotiators who are accountable (held responsible) for their outcomes may be at greatest risk for harboring faulty fixed-pie perceptions. For example, negotiators who feel accountable for their outcomes are more likely to hold the faulty fixed-pie perception when negotiating with an *in*-group member than with an *out*-group member.[7] Why? When people are under pressure to perform with someone from their own team, they tend to be more close-minded and inattentive to new information.

Consider how a manufacturing company COO named "Mark" found the sweet spot after being trapped in a lose-lose situation. In this case, Mark was responsible for a large-scale operating system change. However, several VPs actively sought to block the change when they discovered the details of the new performance radar it included; this baffled Mark because the executives had initially been extremely enthusiastic and supportive of the plan. After several months of stalemate and frustration, Mark initiated a meeting with one of the VPs and learned that they feared the new operating system change would expose their teams' poor performance. Apparently, the VPs had been taking heat on this issue for quite some time. This gave Mark an idea: implement the operating system change, but get the poor performance indicators off the radar.

With some adjustments, Mark was able to place the focus on the efficiencies that the company would quickly realize—i.e., the glass was "half-full" rather than "half-empty." When Mark took the poor performance indicators out of the direct spotlight and helped the VPs save face, the operating program became effective—even helping to boost the lagging teams' performance. In this way, the entire company was able to find the sweet spot, and realize significant gains.

Most negotiations are not purely fixed-sum; in fact, the majority of negotiations are variable-sum, meaning that if parties work together, they can create more joint value than if they are purely competitive. This is the idea of synergy—that the whole can be greater than the sum of the parts. Few conflicts are purely win or lose.[8] The gains of one party do not represent equal sacrifices by the other. This also applies to our personal relationships!

To emphasize, rarely are conflict and negotiation situations purely competitive. Rather, most are *mixed-motive* in nature, meaning that parties' interests are imperfectly correlated with one another. In most mixed-motive situations, people have two incentives vis-à-vis the other party: cooperation (so that they can reach an agreement and avoid stalemate) and competition (so that they can achieve their most desired terms).

For example, consider how one couple (Chris and Pat) found the sweet spot in what seemed to be an intractable relationship conflict. Chris had a dream of competing in an international master's athlete event. Moreover, Chris wanted the moral support of Pat during the week of the event. However,

Pat was reluctant to give up a week to essentially serve as a "support crew." "What's in it for me?" Pat bluntly asked. Chris thought about the orange story and Pat's own life passion: Italian cooking. Chris made a few phone calls and found an Italian chef who could organize a customized, onsite "foodie" experience for the week of the event. After a great deal of organizing, Chris created a "win-win week" where he was able to compete in the athletic event guilt-free, and Pat had the culinary experience of a lifetime. Most importantly, they were able to be together for that week, supporting each other.

Another couple my colleagues and I know was in a similar bind. In this case, one spouse was growing angry about the time her partner invested in training for the event. They reached a win-win agreement when the spouse-in-training agreed to put in all his training hours prior to 8:00 a.m. each day (including weekends) and also to host a number of family brunch events, thereby guaranteeing he would be home in time to prepare the food and serve the guests. He even purchased an industrial-strength headlight that allowed him to train in the dark!

CHAPTER FOUR

Why We Need Sweet Spot Hacks

DANIELLE AND JERRY MET IN MEDICAL SCHOOL SOME YEARS ago and fell madly in love. They married, forming a two-physician family. Danielle finished her residency and took a job at a prestigious university as instructor of medicine—making about $85,000 a year. Meanwhile, Jerry secured a coveted fellowship that offered invaluable experience but, alas, minimal salary. With two young children to care for, Danielle and Jerry made things work because Danielle had a more flexible schedule and was able to walk to work, freeing her to do more for the kids, which she loved.

One day, Jerry came home and announced that his department chair "strongly" recommended he pursue a position at a top oncology residency program in a different state. "Wait just a darn minute!" Danielle said. "I have a life here and I'm not about to leave my walk-to-work job and move to a different state!" Jerry pleaded, "I've always dreamed of doing a residency at a world-class oncology center!" For several weeks, the couple was at an impasse, contemplating the worst—physical separation, two households, divorce?

Finally, Danielle made a proposal: "Look, the most important thing for me is a daily routine that I can manage easily. So give me your top ten oncology programs in the United States, and I'll determine the rank order that you submit." Danielle went on to explain that her rank order would factor in cost of childcare, proximity to relatives, climate, and a number of other factors that were key for her. Jerry agreed. In this way the couple was able to find the sweet spot: Jerry let Danielle have control over the destination, and Jerry was able to pursue his dream of a world-class oncology program.

On my quest to understand the dynamics of the sweet spot, once I established the existence of the fixed-pie perception, I set out to try to debunk it in people. I designed investigations that involved negotiation simulations in which sweet spot arrangements (akin to the sisters and orange from Chapter One, and Danielle and Jerry here) were available, and then examined when and how people overcome the debilitating fixed-pie perception to find the sweet spot.

Ugh! This proved much, much harder than I ever imagined it would. At first, nearly everything I did failed. The fixed-pie perception was so strong! It was not enough to warn people about its existence. Simply encouraging people to practice did not help either. Even providing feedback after several practice sessions didn't fully eliminate it.

Fortunately, some of what I was experimenting with and what other colleagues were studying in their social science research labs started to show promise, refining our understanding. I want to share those important breakthroughs with you and convince everyone—whether you are a manager, executive, business owner, spouse, parent, neighbor, or community member—that these strategies can work for you.

I call these tools "hacks" because they can be employed immediately and don't require a lot of monetary investment, training, expensive consultants, or industry-specific expertise. Before we can make these hacks work, we need to lay the groundwork for getting the most out of them. Four "keys" are important here.

Key One: Belief

First and foremost, people need to believe that they can use the hacks. In some sense, we need to know that *nurture can triumph over nature*. This is important because when it comes to skill with conflict and negotiation, most people are strict naturists. "You've either got it or you don't," they say. "You're either born with it, or you aren't." And the conversation usually stops there. Most people believe that negotiation skills are mostly inherited and fixed, and this stops them from attempting to learn and perform better.

Dr. Laura Kray and her colleague demonstrated how nurture can triumph over nature in an intriguing study. Kray led people to believe that being successful in negotiation was due either to genetic gifts (i.e., nature) or to hard work and effort (i.e., nurture).[1] The *naturists* have *fixed* mindsets—you either have it or you don't. Conversely, *nurturists* have *growth* mindsets—they believe you can develop skills. Her results pointed to a self-fulfilling prophecy. When people adopted a fixed mindset, they were *less likely* to reach sweet spot deals. Conversely, when they adopted a growth mindset, and viewed negotiation as a challenge, they were more successful in reaching high-quality deals. People who believe that negotiation ability can be improved with experience and practice are more likely to discover sweet spot agreements than are people who believe that negotiation skills are not teachable.[2]

I've also conducted a lot of research in which I measure people's ability to find the sweet spot over time. What I've learned is that most people see measurable improvements when they deliberately practice. However, some types of training are much more conducive to learning than others. The least effective method is "lecture-style" training. In fact, nearly any type of role-play training is more effective than lecture-based training![3]

In another investigation, we pitted several different "learning" methods against one another.[4] Specifically, we examined didactic learning (lecture-style learning), learning via information revelation (letting people know what the other party's value drivers were after-the-fact), analogical learning (giving people examples of other sweet spot deals), and observational learning (wherein they observed a "model" group reach a sweet spot deal). We tested the impact of each of these methods experimentally by observing people's performance in negotiations. Hands down, observational learning and analogical learning led to more sweet spot deals than did lecture-style learning! Didactic learning was essentially worthless! Interestingly, negotiators in the observation group showed the largest increase in performance, but the least ability to articulate the learning principles that helped them improve, suggesting that they had acquired tacit knowledge that they were unable to verbalize.

Key Two: Easy to Use

A second key is to realize that learning the hacks won't take a PhD or years of study. Most people believe that it takes years to become a seasoned negotiator. Some people believe that even years of training won't cut it—you have to be born with it—and unless you are in a category with Welch, Buffet, or another archetypal CEO, well, just hang it up.

One reason sweet spot skills training can be challenging is that people believe it will require a lot of effort and deplete their mental reserves. This is why people often want an "easy" solution to a problem. Case in point: One investigation introduced negotiation strategies to learners framed as either "easy" or "difficult." *In actual fact, the strategies were exactly the same.* The negotiators who were told the strategies were "easy" were more likely to successfully adopt the strategy and achieve sweet spot outcomes than were those for whom the same strategy was framed as "difficult."[5]

As a testament to the "easy-to-use" maxim, I encourage my students to put the "best practices" we introduce in class into place immediately. In one situation, a student in my class scheduled a salary negotiation with his company (via conference call) right after the class was scheduled to end. The next day, he told me that he was able to get the company to increase his salary offer by 8 percent, and double his vacation days (from two to four weeks). Moreover, he negotiated a January vacation, which is during a "blackout" period in his industry when almost no one can take time off.

Key Three: Forget Conventional Wisdom

Third, it's important to set aside some assumptions (and conventional wisdom) that many of us have been given. Many of the proven hacks here are nearly the opposite of what common advice dictates!

For example, one of the most common pieces of folklore advice is to "let the other party" talk first in a business negotiation. But scientific research suggests just the opposite! Namely, in most negotiation situations, there is a clear first-mover advantage.[6] Why?

By "going first" or putting the first proposal on the table, negotiators effectively "anchor" the negotiation in their favor, by setting an initial number or focal term. My research on gender and negotiation performance with Laura Kray and Adam Galinsky, for example, shows that women do much better when they make the first offer in a business negotiation.[7] Moreover, when both parties expect the other party to talk first, it leads to an unproductive standoff where neither party is showing their cards.

Another piece of conventional wisdom is to "split things down the middle." Hmm, we've already seen that when people (like the sisters and the orange) divide things equally, this does not lead to win-win because people don't necessarily value the same things. From a very young age, children are taught to divide things equally. Moreover, when people resist equal division, they risk social censure. As a case in point, think about the last time you were part of a large group dinner and the decision was to evenly divide the bill. In a similar situation, one student dinner-goer—knee-deep in student loans and on a tight budget—deliberately did not order the $14-per-glass wine and declined dessert. Yet, when the bill came, the group's quick decision was to simply ask the waitstaff divide the total by seven! When the student protested, the group teased him for being "cheap."

A dinner bill is one thing. What about really high-stakes situations such as long-term work assignments? One biotech firm manager we know set aside conventional wisdom when she was appointed to a new leadership role. She was responsible for allocating research funding for her team. Rather than simply giving each team member an equal budget (treating it like a dinner bill), she asked some questions about needs and quickly realized that resources other than money were also considered to be of great value, including laboratory time. Apparently, there was stiff competition for laboratory equipment on certain days and hours. So, she created a plan in which the team members who got the most desirable lab time received less money, and the members who were more flexible with lab time received more funds.

Key Four: Be Ready to Fail

Finally, and perhaps most importantly, we need to be ready to fail. Psychologist Roger Schank knew that for real learning to occur, people had to come face-to-face with failure.[8] *Expectation failure theory* suggests that when our tried-and-true behaviors don't work, then (and perhaps only then) do we rethink the problem and come up with another solution. To be sure, most of the business managers that I work with are not encountering failure in their negotiations, or at least don't think they are!

After failure occurs, two things need to happen: (1) reflection and feedback, and (2) trying a different strategy or game plan. First, it's important to reflect and think about each conflict and negotiation situation. Indeed, negotiators who reflect upon and think about what happened do much better than those who don't. I learned this lesson myself in the executive classroom years ago. Prior to arriving at the Kellogg School of Management, I was a full-time faculty member in the Psychology Department at the University of Washington. My carefully crafted lecture notes and summary slides worked fine when I was teaching undergraduates, but on the first day of teaching in the business school, a student approached me after class and said, "You know, you're treating us like undergraduates. All of us have business experience and we can make contributions." Rattled and dismayed, I went home and thought about what the student had said and realized that I needed to change my style—immediately!—to suit my new audience. That's the second critical post-failure activity: changing your game plan. It took me well over two years to improve significantly—and I'm still on a learning curve. But the key was to fall flat on my face (yes, my teaching ratings were well below average that first semester, confirming that student's perception) and slowly start to improve.

Moreover, people who adopt *learning* goals vs. *performance-only* goals are more successful. Consider how a leader might activate a learning goal instead of a traditional performance goal. In one investigation, students were given a very complex, stressful organizational task that involved strategic decision-making, productivity analysis, and job assignment.[9] One group was told that the task would measure their basic underlying leadership capabilities. Another group was told that management and leadership skills are developed through practice, and that this task would give them an opportunity to cultivate their capabilities. In fact, both groups went on to complete identical tasks—the only difference was how the task was framed for them. The results were dramatic. The groups that focused on learning and growth actually learned more. They also embraced feedback better, altered their strategies more effectively, and enjoyed the experience more than the other group, in which members were presumably anxious about evaluation of their innate capabilities. The message? How we frame stressful situations can literally alter the way our brain processes information.

If you are willing to embrace these four learning keys, then using the sweet spot hacks will be straightforward and even *fun!* In life, we encounter many situations rife with conflict or potential conflict. The ones that frustrate and stymie us most are challenging situations in our personal lives, such as those involving spouses, children, other family members, and friends—interactions where the relationship stakes are immeasurably high. Another setting ripe for conflict is the workplace, where we might find ourselves in battle with colleagues or seated at the bargaining table facing a customer or client. Still another, increasingly common interaction is the large number of virtual communications in which we engage daily—when the other person is not physically present and we communicate via email, text, chat, or some other technology-enabled means. In the following chapters, I introduce sweet spot hacks for personal, business, and virtual life. All of the hacks have a strong basis in research, and I illustrate each with broad-ranging, illustrative examples from real-life situations I've observed, heard about, or been part of myself. I'm excited to introduce you to these hacks and show you how to use them effectively in all life arenas!

CHAPTER FIVE

Sweet Spot Hacks for Relationships

MY FAVORITE SOCIAL SCIENCE RESEARCH STUDY INVOLVED newlyweds and dating couples—with members of each couple on opposite sides of the negotiating table. Whenever I mention the study in class, my students smile then quickly wince. In this particular investigation, people engaged in a conflict negotiation that had a *non-obvious* sweet spot solution—much like the sisters-and-orange situation.[1] To be sure, the couples' interests *appeared* to be completely opposed, but actually were not—meaning that it was possible to create a win-win agreement. The key question was whether couples could get past their (erroneous) fixed-pie perceptions and find the sweet spot by discovering the hard-to-see win-win agreement.

This is where things got interesting. The study was conducted with two groups of people, the first group of participants were newlyweds and dating couples; they loved each other and obviously felt a lot of empathy toward their partners. The second group was a control group: complete strangers that had never met each other, had no history, and, most likely, no future together. Which group would be more likely to find the sweet spot, the lovers or the strangers?

Most of my students correctly predicted that the strangers did a much better job than the lovers in terms of finding the sweet spot! Indeed, the newlyweds were much more likely to cut the orange in half and walk away half-satisfied, whereas the strangers felt more comfortable exploring and considering several options.[2] This exploration put them on a path to finding the win-win.

Years earlier, a similar study of married couples and mixed-sex, ad hoc dyads (strangers) revealed similar findings: Married couples were more cooperative than were ad hoc couples and reached agreements more quickly, but their outcomes were of lower joint value—i.e., more sour, less sweet![3]

So, why are the couples so reluctant to explore and so quick to agree? The key reason is that partners believe that asking questions, pushing the issue, and rejecting the first proposal might damage their relationship and insult the other party. In short, the very factors that strangers use to chart a path to win-win are regarded as risky by the couples, who believe that their relationships might suffer if they pursue them: "It's not worth disrupting the relationship"; "I want to have a good weekend at home and not upset my spouse."

When we discussed this study in class, one of my executives—a VP of a major company—recounted a situation in which she went out to dinner with her spouse. After they finished a meal at a local Italian restaurant one busy weekend, it became obvious to both that each would have preferred going to the new Asian fusion place down the street. However, they did not realize this until it was too late and ended up at their mutual second choice. (I've had other couples tell me about entire vacations that were, upon reflection, examples of cutting-the-orange in half rather than an elegant win-win). The reaction is always the same: "We love each other—how did we miss the sweet spot?"

Spouses and lovers are one thing. What about friends? My colleagues and I started to wonder whether friends would fall prey to the same lose-lose agreements that the newlyweds did. Would the friends end up like the lovers did, or could they find the sweet spot? So, at the University of Washington I conducted research on how friends negotiate. In our research, my colleagues and I examined how teams of friends negotiated, compared to teams of strangers.[4] Teams of friends would seem to have much more going for them than pairs of people with no working relationship: shared history, similar views, mutual understanding, and above all, trust. However, teams of friends did not make for a formidable front at the negotiating table. In fact, they quickly settled for middle-of-the-road outcomes, presumably so they would appear to their friend as a nice and reasonable person.

In general, there are several documented examples of the "mismanagement of agreement" as seen in the examples above—namely, that people actively avoid conflict, to the point of not expressing their authentic desires and, as a result, end up in a lose-lose scenario. The classic example of the lose-lose effect is the Abilene Paradox.[5] As a Texan, I enjoy sharing this story with my managers—who have come to me to learn how to have "fierce conversations" in their own companies, lest they keep cutting oranges in half.

For those of you not familiar with Jerry Harvey's Abilene Paradox, consider the following:[6]

Imagine piling into a steamy car on a 104-degree west Texas afternoon, tempted by the best ice cream in Texas at the other end of a long fifty sunbaked miles across a flat and dust-blown landscape. Your group seems enthusiastic, and says so even though at home it is tolerable with fans, cold drinks, and games. The best ice cream on a hot day: Who wouldn't go for that?! But after the sunbaked trip to the ice cream shop in Abilene, the flavors on hand are bland—vanilla and an uninspiring chocolate—and neither are as good as remembered. Silence descends as the ice cream is eaten. Hours later, after a return trip across the dusty semi-desert, you arrive back home. No one says anything until you break the silence. "Great trip, right?" you say. "Honestly, no," a friend pipes up, adding that she felt pressured into the trip. "What?!" says another friend. "I went along with it because it seemed like everyone else wanted to go. Who'd want to go fifty miles for ice cream in that heat?" In other words, three people had taken a hundred-mile round trip for ice cream on a 104-degree day, even though they did not want to do so, because they thought that's what the other people in the group wanted to do.

The story of the Road to Abilene epitomizes the notion that among family and friends, conflict is to be avoided at all costs, even if it means a lose-lose outcome for all involved. The need for friends to maintain the illusion of agreement means that differences in preferences, interests, and beliefs are often downplayed or buried. Paradoxically, it is precisely these kinds of differences that would enable negotiators in personal relationships to fashion value-added trade-offs and reach win-win agreements! *The takeaway: friends and colleagues need a way to make their differences known so they can capitalize on them in a win-win fashion.*

In the case of the Abilene Paradox, the sweet spot was to stay home and enjoy the light breeze on the porch. However, in a desperate attempt to be cordial and accommodating, the group's collective sacrifice made them completely miss the sweet spot!

What can possibly explain why people who put their relationship above everything else cut oranges in half, eat Italian when they don't want to, and vacation at their mutual second-choice destination? People who love each other should have deep knowledge of the desires, predilections, and passions of the other party. It's true that people prefer to avoid conflict with loved ones as a general principle, but to prevent those costly and unrewarding trips to Abilene, we need to really understand what traps people fall into in such interactions. I present four such traps below.

Four Lose-Lose Traps

There are four traps that people who love each other can unknowingly fall into when they are attempting to solve conflicts and reach sweet spot deals. The first step is recognizing which trap you are in, based on the descriptions below.

Trap #1: Don't Rock the (Relationship) Boat

Most people in long-term relationships embrace a mindset that says that pursuing our individual interests will come at the direct expense of the relationship, so the best course of action is to dampen or squelch our true desires. The problem with the "don't-rock-the-boat" trap is that people quickly settle for middle-of-the-road solutions, but often feel resentful. Over time, the resentment may build up and spill over to affect the relationship deeply.

One of the fundamental beliefs that people hold in intimate relationships is that the relationship should be communal, not transactional. "Communal" means that there should not be a direct exchange of costs and benefits, such as in a market-type relationship, but rather a selfless attention to the needs of the party.

Unfortunately, few people are capable of showing such selflessness. Even fewer are capable of never keeping score. In fact, a lot of evidence shows that people in even the most intimate relationships are constantly performing a mental accounting of how much they are giving and getting. In personal relationships, the unwritten expectation is that people should be attentive to their partner's needs, but not be concerned with their contributions.[7] For example, in one investigation, pairs of friends and pairs of strangers completed a joint task. A light they saw signaled that the partner either needed help or had made a substantial contribution to the joint task. When the other person was a friend, people looked more at the light that signaled "needs," presumably to be ready to respond to a partner's needs; however, when the person was a stranger, people attended more to the light that signaled inputs—a type of "score-keeping." This suggests that friends and lovers should focus on needs, not on what the other party is bringing to the table. That is, people in close personal relationships should be attentive to *needs* (okay: "I can't lift this box, honey.") but they shouldn't keep track of *contributions* (not okay: "Did you notice that I cleaned the refrigerator?").

Turns out it's not that simple. When people in relationships are asked point-blank about their and their partners' contributions, we see a different story. Namely, most people see their own contributions as more generous than what their partner gives them credit for. This is known as the "egocentric bias effect." Scorecards, in this context, are often not a reflection of objective reality, but instead are self-serving ways of looking at relationship history. For example, one investigation asked couples to indicate the percentage of work they did on a number of household chores and obligations, including paying bills and emptying the dishwater.[8] When added together, the couples' self-claimed percentages totaled dramatically over 100 percent, meaning that each person gave themselves credit for doing well over 50 percent of the work, on average!

The egocentric bias effect is even more rampant in workplace and business situations. For example, in one investigation, some people worked on grading exams.[9] The people who graded many exams in a fixed amount of time argued that remuneration should be based on work accomplished (i.e., how many exams were graded). The people who worked the longest hours argued that remuneration should be based on time invested! Both parties had a hard time acknowledging the legitimacy of the others' arguments because they were blinded by egocentric bias!

When people are keeping score of what they've contributed and received in the relationship and their perceptions are egocentric, it means that at any given time one or both parties are feeling underappreciated. Most people put such feelings aside for periods of time, but at some point the mental accounting system cries "foul" and people seek retribution.

One form of retribution is known as the *spillover effect*. This refers to situations in which people take their aggression and resentment regarding a prior situation and apply it to a new situation, acting in an extreme fashion.[10] The most common type of spillover occurs when the unappreciated party erupts suddenly and their partner is dazed and confused by the out-of-proportion response. This is direct spillover. However, indirect spillover can occur as well, such as when the underappreciated person takes their resentment out on a third party. Indeed, our feelings about prior negotiations with people not only affect how we interact with that person in the future, but influence how we negotiate even with completely different people!

Consider this subtle example of spillover told by my student, Peter. Peter wanted to negotiate with his wife regarding a Sunday golf outing with the guys. So, earlier in the week, Peter was particularly "wonderful" at home and offered to pick up kids, do dishes, and even fold the laundry, something his wife typically did. On Saturday night, Peter reminded his spouse that he had done the laundry and the carpooling that week. This might have not been so bad, except he had kept Post-it notes of these chores and showed them to her to make his case. Rather than agreeing to the outing, his wife tore up the notes and stormed out of the room yelling, "We don't keep score in this house!" Later, Peter learned that his wife would have gladly agreed to his golf outing had he just asked without reminding her of the list of chores he had done that week. Specifically, what upset her was learning that his helpfulness earlier in the week was calculated rather than heartfelt. She thought he was simply attending to her needs, so she was understandably furious when she learned he was only making those contributions so that he could cash in!

Indeed, not rocking the boat often involves stockpiling and scorecards. Meaning that at some point, the taking-one-for-the-team adds up and people begin to feel resentful, fueled by a sense of "You owe me one" or "It's your turn now."

Trap #2: Relational Accommodation

Professor Emily Amanatullah offers a compelling explanation of the fateful lovers and friends effect described above—she calls it "unmitigated communion"—suggesting that friends (and lovers) put their relationship first, so much so that they make immediate and complete sacrifices to save the relationship.[11] People who believe that relationships entail unmitigated communion essentially believe that people in relationships should not keep scorecards and should be completely responsive to the needs of their partner, putting aside their own self-interest.[12] This certainly sounds like a recipe for eliminating relationship conflict. But it also sounds like a mandate to halve oranges, with constant self-sacrifice! We've interviewed several dozen managers and leaders who all admitted that they "took one for the team" because they believed that was best for the relationship.

The problem is that most people are not completely sure what the other spouse wants, but they dare not ask (presumably because they are supposed to know, or should know *if they loved you* . . .) and so they make a guess. More often than not, they're wrong.

Indeed for most of us, the idea of behaving in a self-interested fashion, or selfishly with a friend, is intolerable, so we second-guess their desires (e.g., "I bet he wants Italian"), put a lid on our own preferences ("I'm not going to mention the fusion place I want to go to"), and end up with half an orange!

Unmitigated communion, then, refers to the idea that people believe they should be completely responsive to their partner's needs and not assert their own. This makes sense because most friendships are built on communal norms, which prescribe that we should take care of people we love, respond to their needs and, above all, not keep score of who has put in what.

However, all too often, people engage in relational accommodation when they find themselves in conflict in their personal relationships—meaning that they make personal sacrifices in order to "save" and "preserve" the relationship.[13]

People in relationships believe that accommodating the other party is the best way to express love, caring, and affection. Relational accommodation occurs when people make economic sacrifices to preserve relationships. In a study with researcher Susan Crotty, I explored whether people's greatest source of regret was not following their "heart" or not following their "head" when it came to conflict in their personal relationships. We found that people who regret "not following their heart" often give up more resources than do those who regret "not following their head" because they sacrifice for the relationship. Bottom line: when we listen too much to our hearts, we suppress our own desires and needs and cut the orange in half![14]

A fascinating series of studies crafted by Professor Jared Curhan at MIT took the relational accommodation phenomenon one step further to reveal how couples often make such deep sacrifices that there is no orange left at all![15] Curhan's motivation was the classic O. Henry story, "The Gift of the Magi."[16] In the tragic story, a poor married couple, desperately in love, wants to buy each other a luxurious Christmas gift.

Unable to afford an expensive gift, the wife cuts her long, beautiful hair to buy her husband a watch fob. Meanwhile, the husband sells his watch to buy his wife expensive hair combs. The couple each sacrificed one of their most treasured possessions to please and surprise the other, acts of pure altruism. Unfortunately, though well-meaning, they completely missed the sweet spot.

Curhan figured out how to study the "O. Henry Effect" in commonplace business and personal situations. In one simulation, people participated in an employment negotiation. The job candidate in the simulation took the role of a middle manager seeking a transfer from one branch to another. The person on the other side of the table was the vice president of the targeted branch. Secretly, the situation contained a sweet spot, meaning the manager and VP had similar preferences. Here was the twist: Some of the job candidates were led to believe that the company had an "egalitarian" culture; whereas others were told the company had a "hierarchical" culture. The hypothesis was that when people believe that the company's values are "egalitarian," they are more likely to take one for the team and capitulate, instead of voicing their interests. That is exactly what happened. People operating in the "egalitarian" culture missed the sweet spot in an ill-fated attempt to "be nice and reasonable." Meanwhile, those operating in the "hierarchical" culture felt more comfortable persisting, and were much more likely to create win-win, sweet spot deals.

Most of our personal relationships are characterized by the "egalitarian" norm, not the hierarchical norm. Highly "relational" contexts induce people to forfeit their own interests, take one for the team, and cut the orange in half. We need a hack!

Trap #3: I Am Resilient, But They Are Fragile

Why are couples and friends so concerned about affronting the other party? The answer may have to do with a disconnect between how sensitive we are versus how sensitive *we think others are*. In my research with Dr. Tanya Menon, we found that people believe that others are much more sensitive than they themselves are—kind of a double standard.[17] This essentially amounts to a mindset of, "I can take it, but I must treat others with kid gloves." We called this mindset "threat immunity," such that people essentially see themselves as much tougher than others. To test this idea, we set up a situation in which people were asked to predict how upset others would be versus how upset they themselves would be upon receiving negative feedback, before delivering such feedback. Most people said that they would be completely fine receiving negative feedback but that others would be very upset; so their best course of action in giving such feedback would be to "soften the blow." This of course led to strangely muted, coded messages that became increasingly hard for recipients to understand—the result of that double standard–based thinking.

There are two negative consequences of the "threat immunity" finding. First, the more a person feels that they are immune to threats but others are fragile, the more they "dumb down" their messages to others. This leads to a patronizing communication style in which we are essentially taking pity on others and cloaking our real message. Consider the performance review process, where the idea is to improve people's performance by providing clear, constructive feedback. However, people are afraid others may "fall apart" or get angry in the face of personal criticism, so they overcompensate and deliver ambiguous, watered-down messages that leave the recipient feeling confused, especially if it's face-to-face. For example, superiors give more blunt feedback when they do it in writing versus in person.[18]

The other negative consequence is that the greater our feeling of threat immunity, the less connection and rapport we develop in our relationships. Bottom line: We start to disconnect from the very people we are trying to be close to! Tanya Menon and I measured this disconnect in our research investigation by asking people how satisfied they were with the outcome of their discussion and with the relationship itself. A strange and disturbing pattern appeared: the more people believed that they "threatened" others, the more their relationship with the other party suffered. What this essentially amounted to is that people who falsely believe that they threaten others are more likely to coddle others and dumb down their communications, which has the unintended effect of disrupting the very relationship they are concerned about. The solution, then, is to stop yourself from believing that your talent, beauty, and skills are threatening to others and instead reflect on how talented and strong that other person really is, to have more equal-feeling interactions.

Observing findings like those above, my colleagues and I decided to measure just how thin-skinned people really are.[19] The technical term for this is "face threat sensitivity." To measure face threat sensitivity, we asked people three questions: How thin-skinned are you? Are your feelings easily hurt? Do you not take criticism well? Indeed, we found that some people are naturally more sensitive or thin-skinned than others, and when they are threatened it can lead to particularly poor outcomes. People who reported being easily threatened were more competitive and less likely to reach agreement and find the sweet spot. In short, the more easily insulted or hurt another person is, the worse the outcome is for everyone.

Trap #4: Indirect Communication

When we think others are fragile, we are constantly "editing," carefully monitoring our words and behaviors so as not to insult, anger, or frustrate the other person, who in actual fact is most likely treating us the same way. This "editing" leads to a strange communication dynamic in which both partners cloak their language, hiding what they really think in much longer, carefully hedged, ambiguous terms that would be hard even for a linguist to decipher! Such hedging language is known as "indirect communication."

One investigation studied the incidence and fallout of indirect communication.[20] The question was how direct versus indirect people are in their communication. Interestingly, the study concluded that when we communicate with complete strangers, we often use a direct communication style. We become even more direct if we think that person may be unfamiliar with the situation or context, such as with a newcomer in the area or a new hire at work. However, we communicate in a much more indirect fashion with people we are familiar with.

In another study, the question focused on whether the receiving party understood the message and how many cognitive steps it took to get there.[21] Most people believe that they communicate better with close friends than with strangers. However, the study found that closeness led people to overestimate how well they communicate—a phenomenon known as the "closeness-communication bias."[22] For example, people who attempted to follow instructions communicated by a friend were more likely to make egocentric errors—look at and reach for an object only they could see—than when they were given directions by a complete stranger! And, when people attempted to convey a particular meaning in an ambiguous phrase, they overestimated their success more when communicating with a friend or spouse than with a stranger. Why? People engage in more active monitoring of strangers' messages because they know they must, but they "let down their guard" and rely more on their own perspective when they communicate with a friend.

Indirect communication requires several more cognitive steps on the part of the receiver to figure out what the sender is really trying to say. For example, take the case of a couple in which one spouse wants the other to close the door.[23] The most direct request would be "Close the door." But consider how the same request might be embedded in less direct messages such as "When will you close the door?" or "It's cold in here" or even "I don't want the cats to get out of the house."

Indirect communication gives us an "out" if our relational partner seems upset. That enables us to adjust our intent after the fact, to fit the situation—a type of plausible deniability wherein a person can deny that their comment or request was made, because it wasn't made directly. But it also decreases the likelihood that the other person will actually understand the message's true meaning.

When it comes to criticism or delivering bad news, people are particularly likely to "cloak" their messages. For example, a study of 150 people who carried out acts of apologizing, complaining, refusing, and thanking revealed marked differences in directness depending upon what message they needed to convey. While participants generally expressed the acts of thanking, apologizing, and refusing explicitly, they performed the act of complaining mostly implicitly.[24]

Using indirect speech may appear to be very kind and humane, but when we attempt to "soften the blow" we distort the message, requiring the receiver to essentially play detective and figure out the signal through all of the noise. It can be very difficult for perceivers to understand what the sender means, and thus people often end up in a lose-lose situation because the message is never received as intended.

In one case, a husband bought an expensive necklace and earrings made from reclaimed bicycle parts for his wife. This may seem like a strange gift, but his wife was an avid triathlete. So the husband thought it made a "perfect" gift for her. But she hated the jewelry—it was heavy, difficult to fasten, and left a mark on her skin. Upon receiving the unique gift, she was touched that he had put such careful thought into it and said "Thank you," but never wore the pieces, hoping that would send a signal. Apparently he didn't notice the indirect "I'm not wearing this stuff" because, to her horror, on their next anniversary he proudly presented her with two "reclaimed bicycle parts" bracelets! She groaned, thinking about how she would "break his heart" by saying anything negative—not to mention that he was "breaking the bank" with the unwanted gifts. With Valentine's Day just around the corner, though, she mustered the courage to have a direct conversation. "Honey, I know Valentine's Day is coming up. I don't need more jewelry. I do need a new suitcase for my upcoming trip, though." She held her breath, but he smiled and said, "Come to think of it, I've never seen you wear the others!"

What about direct communication when the stakes are much higher, such as a couple struggling to get along? The answer depends on whether partners are able and willing to change. Direct communication is beneficial when couples have serious problems that need to be addressed and partners are able to change; however, direct communication can be harmful when partners are not confident or secure enough to be responsive.[25] By contrast, less direct communication that involves showing affection and validation may be beneficial when problems are minor, cannot be changed, or involve partners whose defensiveness curtails problem-solving.

Compounding this issue in general is that we overestimate our directness. Sometimes, for example, we think we are being direct but the other party does not know what we mean. This can happen when we (falsely) believe that the other person is aware of the same information that we are. We know what we mean, we think the other person knows what we mean, but the perceiver is confused or unsure. This is known as the *illusion of transparency*: The sender thinks they are being clear and kind, but the receiver is baffled.[26] The result is pluralistic ignorance—no one really knows what is understood or what the true meaning of the communication is. This happens all too often in many relationships where one spouse attempts to communicate something to the other and is convinced they "get the message," but in reality the message is lost or not received as intended.

Business partners are often faced with the same type of communication challenge when they need to communicate with one another in a way that a third party (a client, for example) may not understand. This is known as the "multiple audience" problem.[27] In one situation, I was on a team of service-providers that was trying to woo an important client. I arrived to an important conference meeting with the prospect about an hour after it started, so I wasn't privy to the conversation before my arrival. Apparently, before I'd gotten there the client had revealed a very important "must have" that they assumed we had previously acknowledged. Thus it was important for me to mention that specific client need without being explicitly prompted. During the meeting, my team was trying to subtly communicate the client's "must have" to me so that my comments would seem to emerge naturally. But I wasn't getting their signal. I was aware, however, that the conversation was becoming strangely opaque, as my team kept "circling back" to get me to "continue to elaborate." At one point, a teammate obviously realized that I was never going to get it, so she took a risk by writing a short phrase on a pad of paper, almost as if she was doodling. Fortunately, I saw her note after she nudged me under the table, and I understood the message and was able to pivot the conversation to address the client's "must have."

To illustrate the illusion of transparency, in one investigation, people were asked to say a syntactically ambiguous sentence in a way that they were confident that a receiver would understand the message.[28] The sentence was "Angela shot the man with the gun." As you can see, it has two possible meanings: One meaning is that Angela shot a man by using a gun; the other is that Angela shot a man who himself was packing a weapon. Now, let's imagine further that the distinction of these two possible meanings is significant and important, so it's critical to convey the meaning correctly. In the study, most people were very confident about their ability to convey the intended meaning. Despite that, the receivers were baffled, and were wrong about the intended message 50 percent of the time—no better than chance! That's the illusion of transparency at work.

Perhaps not surprisingly, the illusion of transparency is present in many long-term relationships. Couples and business partners with depth of knowledge of the other party believe that others—even those whom they love—are acutely aware of their inner needs, thoughts, and intentions: "They get me. They really do." As we shall see, this kind of excessive self-focus blinds us from finding the sweet spot. A colleague told me it took over a year for her husband and her to mutually realize that she wanted to work full-time and he wanted to be a full-time stay-at-home dad. The realization came when her husband had returned from a grueling business trip and said, "I wish I could have been home this week instead of on the road." She said, "I would have loved that! Because if you would have been here, I could have been working on my business idea!" They joked about the situation for a couple minutes before understanding that they had heartfelt mutual desires that were not being realized in their current situation. They also realized that they could eventually make a "swap" that would result in both of them being much happier. Soon after, she returned to her full-time position and he resigned from his job.

The illusion of transparency was also a wake-up call for "Greta," a high-profile physician I know at a major university hospital. "This explains everything," Greta told me when she learned about the phenomenon in my class. Specifically, she had been struggling with one of her direct reports for months about the steps required for a new hire. Greta was increasingly frustrated because the report could not remember the steps to follow for their recruitment process. Greta had been in her position for well over a decade and had served on several hiring committees, so the steps involved in recruiting new staff were very clear—at least to her. However, each time that a new hire was to be recruited, the direct report seemed not to remember anything.

Once we demonstrated the "illusion of transparency" effect, Greta realized that she had never sat down and given her direct report the big picture. So she took forty-five minutes for a coffee meeting with the report, sharing and explaining the steps involved; she also added a technique she termed "teach me." I asked her how "teach me" worked. Greta explained that after imparting the information to her report, she asked the report to now explain the recruiting steps back to her. She was careful not to position this as a "gotcha test," but prefaced her ask by saying, "I have realized that my communication is not as clear as I want it to be. If you teach me, this will help me improve my own communication skills." The direct report let out a sigh of relief and explained the recruiting process accurately overall, a win-win.

Rethinking Relationship Advice

The common advice offered to people in relationships is geared toward minimizing conflict and keeping the peace. This makes sense on the face of it. However, much of this common wisdom may put unwitting couples, lovers, and families on a path toward slicing oranges in half or worse, having no orange at all!

It's important to critically examine the advice that has crept into our "relationship mental models." In the section below, traditional relationship advice is modified, extended, and, in some cases, turned upside down—all in the name of finding the sweet spot with the people we love the most.

Sweet Spot Hacks for Relationships

Finding the sweet spot in personal relationships is difficult or downright impossible if people are not willing to articulate clearly their true interests and pain points. We are certainly not suggesting that people start making demands and focusing exclusively on their own needs. This is not practical and will probably hurt relationships. The key is to use hacks that allow you to find the sweet spot in the conflicts you're facing in your relationships without putting the relationship at risk.

This chapter introduces nine hacks for finding the sweet spot in personal relationships. Note that on the surface, many of these hacks would seem to be the opposite of what might actually be effective, which is why people so often fail to use them.

HACK 1 >

This Is Your Brain on Empathy

Within the broad universe of relationship advice, showing empathy is probably the most common prescription. "Take a minute to imagine how your partner is feeling" is often encouraged. Psychologist Carl Rogers said that having empathy "means temporarily living in the other's life, moving about in it delicately without making judgments; it means sensing meanings of which he or she is scarcely aware, but not trying to uncover totally unconscious feelings."[29] *Psychology Today* advises "Having empathy can lead to having compassion. When you have compassion for someone else, you want to help them or relieve any suffering they're experiencing. The idea is that you cannot have compassion for another individual unless you actually recognize or understand that they're actually suffering."[30] People are hardwired to be empathic with those closest to them because when we're close with someone, they become part of ourselves.[31] The common folklore is that empathy and being empathic is considered an essential skill for successful relationships. The question here, then, is whether empathy really helps people find the sweet spot.

Well, I was as surprised as you to learn that empathy is not as effective as you might expect in helping people find the win-win in their relationships. In fact, empathy can totally backfire in terms of leading us to the sweet spot. Why? When people focus on how their partner is *feeling*, it may be very comforting but it doesn't help them understand how to rework a frustrating situation into a win-win. For example, consider "Kris" and "Jamie," longtime friends and collaborators. The pair had written several books together and routinely did lucrative public speaking events and consulting as a team, sharing the fees equally. In one situation, Jamie was invited to work solo with a consulting client that had previously engaged both of them, creating a rift between the friends. Seeing Kris's frustration, Jamie made several attempts to be "empathic" and understanding ("I can only imagine how you must be feeling" and "I know that you are upset and I don't blame you"). However, empathy itself wasn't enough to solve the problem, which was affecting the relationship significantly.

The hack? To be sure, we are not suggesting that people become cold and dispassionate. Quite the opposite. The question is how to better envision, develop, and execute a win-win situation. We need an empathy hack!

It turns out that there is a close cousin of empathy that serves as the perfect hack. That cousin is "perspective-taking." Perspective-taking is kind of like empathy, but also has a brain (not just a heart)! Here's the difference: When we *empathize*, we imagine how the other party is *feeling*: sad? hurt? lonely? frustrated? When we engage in *perspective-taking*, we imagine how the other person is *thinking*—perhaps sad because we forgot their birthday; or hurt that we canceled the vacation plans; or, in the case of Kris and Jamie, unappreciated because their intellectual work is not being properly recognized. In the Kris and Jamie situation, Jamie used perspective-taking to realize that Kris's concern was not simply feeling "hurt" but frustration that Kris's intellectual property wasn't being acknowledged, much less remunerated. Jamie was able to use that insight to resolve the situation by agreeing to display Kris's intellectual contributions fully on all printed material for the client and to agree to pay a percentage of the consulting fee to Kris.

In general, thinking about the other person's point of view is more effective in finding the sweet spot than simply trying to feel what the other person is feeling. Thus, perspective-taking is different than pure empathy. Whereas perspective taking is a *cognitive* ability to consider the world from another's viewpoint, empathy is the ability to connect emotionally with another person.[32] To be sure, perspective-taking and empathy are both useful in different types of negotiations: Perspective-taking leads to more accurate understanding of other parties in negotiation, whereas empathy produces greater emotional understanding.[33] Negotiators who either are naturally high in perspective-taking ability or are prompted to take the perspective of the counterparty are more successful in identifying and reaching sweet spot outcomes in negotiation. Perspective-takers are more likely than empathizers to discover hidden sweet spot agreements, achieve maximum joint gains, and secure peace.

Perspective-taking saved the day in a recent conflict I witnessed between a senior leader and a staff member. The senior leader felt that he had complete control over a project; yet the staff member was making unilateral, independent decisions, causing the senior leader to see red. Moreover, each party attributed nefarious motives to the other, believing the other was behaving badly. Inflammatory emails ensued and each party attempted to build a blocking coalition. Early efforts to get these two people to "empathize with the other" backfired, to say the least: "I don't give a damn about how she feels about this situation, she is way out of line" and "What a pompous, entitled control freak he is!"

Needless to say, conflict was quickly spiraling. When each party calmed down enough to engage in a perspective-taking exercise, something very interesting happened. When asked to think about why the staff member was asserting control, the senior leader came to realize that the staff member was attempting to carve out a new job position for herself; making independent decisions and exercising judgment were her ways of building a business case for her desired new role. In a complementary fashion, when the staff member was asked why the senior leader was so adamant about retaining decision control, she realized that the senior leader was planning to step down in the next few years and saw this project as his unique legacy. Following this perspective-taking exercise, the senior leader and staff member crafted a beautiful sweet spot solution: The senior leader made unilateral project decisions, but used his influence to recommend that the staff member be promoted to lead the newly formed initiative.

HACK 2 >>>>>>>>>>>>>>>>>>>>>>>>>>>>>>>>>>>>>>>

Suspicious Minds
(Maybe Elvis Was Wrong . . .)

The other most common piece of relationship advice is "trust your partner." And, if you don't trust your partner, well, that is the beginning of the end. Trust is considered a cornerstone for effective relationships.

Elvis crooned, "We can't go on together with suspicious minds . . ." But the research suggests something a little different: Suspicion may serve us well, or at least better than distrust, when it comes to finding the win-win in our personal relationships. Let me give an example. I do some work with family businesses where emotions, relationships, and the past can often loom large, as would be expected. The word "trust" comes up frequently, as many family business members tell me that they have lost trust in others.

Javier, for example, told me his specific family business situation involved "a lot of love, a lot of history, and a lot of distrust." For years, Javier had felt that his uncle was not being forthcoming with the family business's financial statements. To make matters worse, Javier's father had recently passed away, and there had always been a rivalry between the two brothers. Over coffee with me, Javier expressed deep frustration and a lack of trust for his uncle. "What are you going to do?" I asked. Javier sighed and said, "I may have to leave the business, but I don't want to."

Now, we've got a problem, because trust is really important for finding the sweet spot. But I can't just snap my fingers and tell people like Javier to trust people with whom they've had a breach of trust. So, we need a trust-hack: *transform distrust into suspicion*. When I do this, a lot of my clients and students say, "Distrust and suspicion are the same darn thing!" I wink and suggest that distrust and suspicion are actually quite different.

One leads to lose-lose outcomes and the other can lead to win-wins. Why? When we distrust someone, we have *negative expectations about their motives*—just as Javier had negative expectations about his uncle and even considered withdrawing from his role in the family business.

However, when we are suspicious, we are *uncertain of their motives*. As such, I encouraged Javier to brainstorm a variety of motivations that might explain his uncle's behavior. This was difficult because Javier was so distrustful. Eventually, he was able to consider some alternative explanations, including the possibility that the uncle felt responsible for the family's welfare and did not want anyone to worry about finances. Another explanation Javier considered was that his uncle lacked a formal education and was possibly intimidated by Javier's financial skills acquired in business school, and therefore wanted to avoid appearing ignorant or incompetent.

The reason why suspicion is more effective is that distrust usually leads to withdrawal (or combat), but suspicion can lead to well-meaning questioning. Indeed, when a negotiator is suspicious of their opponent, they are more likely to reach more win-win agreements and find the sweet spot than when they are not suspicious.[34] With our ongoing sisters-and-orange example, it's tempting to imagine how if one sister had been suspicious about the other's intentions or interests, this may have led to a win-win agreement! The bottom line is that trust is great; but don't count on it! If possible, set aside your feelings of distrust and become suspicious and curious. A few months later, Javier told me that he was able to speak with his uncle about the finances in the family business and come to a better understanding of his uncle's motives, enabling Javier to happily stay part of the business.

HACK 3 >>>>>>>>>>>>>>>>>>>>>>>>>>>>>>>>>>>>>>>

I'm Not Angry, I'm Disappointed

Sometimes, not all goes well in paradise. Partners get frustrated and angry. The common prescription is not to repress anger but to express it. Indeed, suppressing anger can create a stress reaction that plays a part in a wide range of psychosomatic ailments, such as headaches, hypertension, cardiovascular disease, and even cancer.[35] Hence the common advice is to express anger. Psychologists and therapists alike encourage people to recognize and accept their angry emotions and learn how to express them in nonthreatening ways.[36] Even the Dalai Lama noted that expressing anger is beneficial: "If a human being never shows anger, then I think something's wrong. He's not right in the brain."[37]

Anger is a common emotion in conflict and negotiation, too. In fact, of all the emotions that threaten people's ability to find the sweet spot, anger is number one. Why? Anger is the emotion that is most often reciprocated, meaning that anger expressed by person A leads to an expression of anger by person B. This of course instigates an escalating "anger arms race," in which angry people are more likely to make threats and the counterparty reciprocates in kind, leading to a conflict spiral. The question, then, is how to extricate yourself from the doom-loop of anger. Well, as you might guess, it simply does not work to admonish people to "calm down" or "not be angry"—if anything, as most of us have experienced, this throws fuel on the fire. So, we need an anger hack.

If you can't take a momentary break or find your own reset button, then the ideal hack to stop an escalating anger-and-attack spiral is the "disappointment hack." Here's why. Not all negative emotions have the same consequences or activate the same brain regions.[38] Unlike anger, disappointment is not a *reciprocal* emotion. Rather, disappointment often generates a *complementary* response such that when Person A expresses disappointment, Person B seeks to mitigate or "fix" the disappointment. On one hand, it may seem that expressing disappointment communicates weakness; on the other hand, it may invite the other party to help. Indeed, one investigation examined how people responded to an opponent who was disappointed or worried, versus their reactions to an unemotional or a guilty-seeming opponent. People conceded more when the opponent was disappointed, and conceded the least when the opponent showed guilt.[39]

I witnessed the complementary reaction of offering help in the face of disappointment firsthand when I was an innocent bystander observing a customer-salesperson encounter at a high-end department store. Okay, I was eavesdropping, but only in the name of research! In this case, the customers were a mother and daughter picking up a graduation dress that the store had altered at their request. However, the mother had recently discovered that the dress was "noncompliant" with the school's (apparently) very strict dress code. More alterations would not remedy the problem. The mother immediately used anger, arguing "any reputable high-end department store should be fully aware of the dress code in the local public high schools," and demanded a full refund. The store clerk cited various terms and conditions that she was literally reading from the fine print on the back of the long receipt, starting most of her sentences with "Unfortunately . . ." Voices were raised and threats hurled back and forth. At that moment, the daughter deployed a brilliant "disappointment" strategy. "Mom," she said, "it's not really her [the sales clerk's] fault. Let's not make this any worse. I'm just so disappointed that my graduation day won't happen the way I wanted it to." In an instant, the clerk's demeanor changed—apparently, she had a daughter, too. And, suddenly, she *wanted to help*. With just a few clicks on her keyboard, she was able to authorize an exchange on the condition that a dress of similar cost was purchased from the store.

In the situation above, as in a lot of conflicts, parties are self-interested and often have little reason to be concerned about the other party. In this case, the clerk wanted to make her sales commissions and avoid extra work, and the mother wanted VIP customer service that may not have been warranted. As it turns out, showing disappointment is particularly effective with people who are highly self-interested. Why? People who are self-interested see disappointment as a threat to getting what they want, and they switch gears to

70

figure out how to achieve their goal, which often results in more mutual benefit.[40]

Don't Look Now (Men, Eye Contact, and Testosterone)

When it comes to conflict, we've all been told to "look people in the eye." Indeed, when someone avoids eye contact, we tend to trust them less and even believe they may be lying. However, eye contact is also a tactic related to power and dominance. Indeed, powerful people and those with status are more likely to stare others down.

Researcher Roderick Swaab wondered whether eye contact could make things worse in certain conflict situations.[41] He reasoned that females are more likely to understand others in the presence of visual contact, but men are more likely to understand others in the absence of such contact. Why? Eye contact is a signal of dominance and aggression. Swaab predicted that men who maintained steady eye contact would act and feel more aggressive. To test that he measured (with permission) participants' testosterone levels. In Swaab's experimental setup, some people negotiated face-to-face and maintained steady eye contact. Other participants did not maintain steady eye contact. Moreover, in some cases men negotiated with men; in other cases, women negotiated with women. Indeed, eye contact led to worse outcomes for males, but not for females, as predicted. The results were definitive: Eye contact did indeed increase testosterone levels in men, ultimately thwarting the effectiveness of the deal.

In fact, when women had direct eye contact they were *more* (not less) likely to find the sweet spot! Why? Women are much more comfortable with eye contact than men—when women make eye contact, they do it to understand others. Men, on the other hand, more typically make eye contact when they want to compete and dominate.

Now, it may be impractical for people to avoid eye contact strategically with others. Indeed, in most business and personal meetings, people are seated in a fashion that may make it hard to avoid such contact. So the hack may need to involve something we can more strategically control: the seating arrangement.

Several studies of group behavior have found that when people are seated closer together, more conversation occurs. People who like each other sit closer together; when strangers sit close together, they are more inclined to like one another.[42]

Seating configuration can activate fundamentally different human needs that, in turn, influence persuasion.[43] When people are seated in a circular layout, for example, they evaluate persuasive material (such as sales pitches) more favorably when it contains family-oriented cues or majority-endorsement information. However, when they are seated in more angular arrangements (such as a square table), they evaluate persuasive material more favorably when it contains self-oriented cues or minority endorsement. Why? Circular seating activates our need to belong, but angular seating activates our need to be unique.

In addition to observing the research investigations on this subject, I've also witnessed it firsthand in my classes. Through some pre-exercise staging, I've experimented with across-the-table seating versus corner-to-corner seating. When people are seated directly across the table from one another, their behaviors are more competitive, and outcomes suffer. However, when they are seated on the edge of the table sides, next to one another in a corner-to-corner fashion, their behaviors are more collaborative and they are more likely to reach sweet spot agreements.

A student in my class shared that when negotiating business deals with clients, she is careful to use only round tables for meetings. On more than one occasion, she chose a restaurant based on its furniture (round versus square/rectangular tables), to strategically influence the nature of the negotiation.

HACK 5 >>>>>>>>>>>>>>>>>>>>>>>>>>>>>>>>>>>>>>>

Don't Go It Alone

One of the most painful research findings that I've uncovered in my studies—which has also been replicated by many others—is that women tend to get worse deals than men when it comes to negotiations of various types.[44] Certainly this is true for salary negotiations; but it is also the case for major purchases, like cars and houses.[45] There are a lot of factors that explain why women tend to get stuck with not-so-sweet deals, including outright bias and the fact that they are often not taken as seriously as men. Not surprisingly, the women I know are more than frustrated by this, and they want a level playing field when it comes to negotiating everything from salaries to vacation time to cars.

Tamara, for example, was a young manager in one of my classes. She recounted a situation in her former position as a consultant in a large firm. Tamara noticed that the men in her practice area—hired at the same time as she—were routinely awarded more attractive engagements and clients. She also discovered that the men enjoyed higher bonuses and salary increases. Yet, try as she might, Tamara could not find a performance-based explanation for this disparity.

When I sat down to speak with Tamara I asked her two questions: (1) How often do you initiate negotiations with senior partners about consulting engagements and salary? (2) When you do, how do you make your case?

Tamara's nonverbal response told me everything. As I suspected, Tamara did *not* opportunistically initiate negotiations; she tended to wait patiently until it was performance-review time. "Ugh, I don't like asking for more!" was her attitude. Meanwhile, the men on her team opportunistically negotiated quite often, and had been engaged in several "ask" discussions with the senior partners. Moreover, when she was involved in a negotiation, Tamara admitted to being very uncomfortable and often retreated on her ask. But she offered an important personal insight that confirmed my thinking: "When I'm asking on behalf of my team or another person, I'm much more assertive."

"Give me an example of that," I said. "Well, last year, my staff was working overtime during tax season to get a report and filing ready for a very important client. They were not getting paid very much, and many of them were only part-time. I wanted to ask the senior partners to increase their hourly wages and pay a bonus, and I had no trouble going to bat for them!"

With that insight, Tamara had stumbled on one of the most effective hacks for carving out a sweet deal. Namely, when you ask for something—whether it's a raise, price reduction, more vacation days, or whatever—*imagine that you are negotiating on behalf of a team or group*. In some cases, this is easy to do—such as in Tamara' case, as she really was trying to protect her team.

But sometimes, we may need to create what I call a "mental constituency." For example, in one research study, some people were told that they were negotiating on behalf of an important "constituency" that was counting on them to come back with a good deal. Other people were not placed under this constituency pressure.[46] These people never met or saw the constituency, but were just informed that they would be accountable at a later point in time. Indeed, people who were accountable to a constituency negotiated better terms for themselves, presumably because they did not want to disappoint that unseen group. However, the findings came with an important caveat. Accountability to a team led to greater sweet spot (win-win) outcomes only when the parties involved expected to interact in the future. Thus the best outcomes were attained when (1) parties anticipated working together in the future and (2) each party represented a group.

What about those of us who don't have a team or constituency that we need to report back to? For example, what about people who are simply trying to negotiate a sweeter compensation package at work? One of my executive students—a woman in a large financial advisory company—solved this creatively. She prepped herself for a negotiation with her senior leader by negotiating on behalf of her "retired self." As the single wage-earner in her household (with a stay-at-home-husband and four kids) she prepared by doing estimates of her net earnings after paying for a combined sixteen years of college education for her children. In the meeting, she even used the pronoun "we," in reference to her current and future selves. It worked: She walked out of the meeting with a very attractive raise.

Another young woman I know, a personal trainer on a fixed income, had her car stolen and needed to purchase a new one fast, so she could get to multiple fitness facilities to meet clients. When she walked into the dealership, she slipped on a fake wedding ring and set her phone alarm sound after forty minutes, so she could take a "call" to consult with her partner about the price and other terms. She was successful in getting what she considered a significant price reduction because she presented herself as the "procurement officer" for her household.

The research findings of Hannah Riley Bowles, Linda Babcock, and Kathleen McGinn reveal that women are particularly likely to craft sweeter deals for themselves when they are representing a group, team, or constituency.[47] Why? Traditionally, women don't feel comfortable asking for more because they risk appearing greedy or entitled, and could meet with backlash. However, when women are representing a constituency or group, they feel more comfortable asking for a sweeter deal on its behalf.

HACK 6 ›››››››››››››››››››››››››››››››››››››

(Give Them) the Silent Treatment

A cornerstone of typical relationship advice is to engage and interact. Indeed, the strong belief is that when couples stop engaging and stonewall or otherwise give one another the "silent treatment," this may well be the beginning of the end.

Perhaps no other type of tactic causes more stress and strife in relationships as the silent treatment, which amounts to not speaking to your partner, not looking at your partner—essentially ghosting your partner, even when they're sitting at the same table as you. Consequently, marital researchers and therapists admonish couples to keep the conversation going and stay closely engaged. Indeed, during my training as a marriage and family counselor, we were strongly urged to maintain engagement, not only between us and our clients, but also to facilitate engagement between our clients and their partners.

For this reason alone, it would seem heretical to advise people in relationships to fall silent and stay that way. Well, MIT researcher Jared Curhan started to wonder whether too much talk might in some sense blind people from seeing sweet spots right in front of them.[48] That is, engaging in constant communication may prevent us from finding a solution.

So, Curhan teamed up with computer scientists who studied thousands of hours of conflict and negotiation discussions. They zeroed in on what they termed "uncomfortably long silences"—or those of about twenty seconds. For most people that is a conversational eternity. A fascinating pattern emerged from the research. Shortly following each uncomfortably long silence, an "orange" was divided in a win-win way. Stated more scientifically, Curhan found a strong relationship between silence and subsequent win-win deals in negotiations and conflict. Curhan then created interesting role-play scenarios in which he strictly cautioned people to be silent for as long as possible in a negotiation. Most people had a hard time with this because that feels tantamount to "checking out." However, the same finding emerged: Prolonged silence led to more win-win outcomes. Curhan then dug deeper and found that periods of silence were associated with greater cognitive activity and creative thinking, thereby producing the sweet spot deal.

Because I'm an applied researcher, I decided to do my own pilot test of the "silent treatment" with my daughter during what was becoming a rather heated conflict about her study abroad travel plans and related budget. This was an ideal conflict negotiation situation to experiment with, because there were so many variables involved—the price of the round-trip tickets, meals, accommodations, and special events, like concerts. I must say that my first attempt to remain quiet did not work so well, as my daughter accused me of "giving her the silent treatment." So I built in a hack to the hack, by offering, "I'm very interested in ensuring that I understand where you are coming from and not losing sight of all these factors, so I'm going to pause for twenty seconds and do my own mental review because I want to make sure that my words actually have real meaning." This seemed to relieve her. After my silent period two things happened: my daughter took her own period of silence, and over the next half hour we resolved the issue. So, my hack was to announce that I was not checking out of the conversation by remaining silent, but rather, doing my own thinking.

HACK 7 >>>>>>>>>>>>>>>>>>>>>>>>>>>>>>>>>>>>

Put Away the *Wall Street Journal*

"If my wife emails you, tell her I'm taking a finance class."

On the first day of a weeklong, live-in executive MBA negotiation course I was teaching, a manager told me that. I looked at him, bewildered, because he was actually enrolled in my *negotiation* course. He explained, "She's worried that I'm going to use the tactics in this class to win arguments in our house. She's really nervous about it." It was clear to me that this student (and his spouse) had a *win-lose* mental model of negotiation. They both viewed "negotiation" as a situation in which there are winners and losers. They're not the only ones who look at negotiation this way.

As I reflected on what my student had told me about his spouse, I realized that I had engaged in similar behavior (i.e., being evasive about the topic I teach) in my own business dealings. Like many people, I've bought and sold my share of houses and properties. When it comes to the innocent question raised by realtors, agents, and principals of "What do you do for a living?" I've learned to never, ever say, "I teach courses in negotiation." Why? Because they immediately put their guard up: "Whoa! That means I shouldn't tell you anything, right?" So my hack is that I simply don't use the word "negotiation." Now, don't get me wrong: I don't lie. I just say that I'm employed by a business school and teach courses in teamwork, conflict management, collaboration, creativity, business, and emotional intelligence—all true!

My colleagues and I wondered whether the very term "negotiation" might cause people anxiety by eliciting for them the competitive aspect of the situation. Perhaps friends negotiating something, for example, might be better able to find the sweet spot if they don't think of it as a "negotiation" but rather a "joint problem-solving situation." So we designed a realistic experiment in which people had to negotiate with a friend, but we referred to the situation with two different names—the ones above. Otherwise everything was the same!

We figured that friends might be very hesitant to "negotiate" against a friend, but much more comfortable engaging in "joint problem-solving." Unbeknownst to the friends seated at the table, the task contained some completely compatible issues—in which their desires were fully aligned. For example, in one case, they were planning a vacation in which several issues needed to be resolved, such as hotel, mode of travel, length of stay, and the season to travel. They had different preferences for most of these issues, but when it came to mode of travel (e.g., airplane, car, train, etc.) they wanted exactly the same thing. The question was whether they would realize this and find the sweet spot, or fail to optimize.

We also measured people's communal orientations prior to negotiation. A person's communal orientation is their beliefs regarding how people in personal relationships should allocate and share resources.[49] People with high communal orientations believe that relationship partners should take care of one another's needs without regard to who may be contributing more. People with low communal orientations treat their friendships more like business transactions, with careful attention to "getting and giving."

So what happened? Friends who viewed the task as a "problem-solving" situation and who were similar in their communal orientation were the most likely to reach sweet spot outcomes.[50] However, when friends were dissimilar in communal orientation, their ability to see win-win opportunities declined precipitously. This meant that when one of the members of the friendship pairs was high in communal orientation but the other was low, they did not land in the sweet spot.

Along the same lines, Kathleen McGinn studied how roommates and friends negotiated, and quickly discovered that the word "negotiation" itself is taboo among these groups.[51] It seems people don't like that word if they are in a relationship. McGinn found that people in relationships would rather use the term "working things out." By studying transcripts of eighty-seven two-party negotiations among friends, she found that most pairs quickly attempted to coordinate a shared logic of exchange, and they essentially engaged in improvisation. This improvisation took one of three forms: *opening up* ("I think in order for us to make the most money it makes sense for us each to tell each other what our numbers are," followed by, "I agree, that's what I'd like to do"), *working together* ("I guess a good way to do it might be to find some kind of midpoint between what I'd be willing to pay and what you would be" followed by, "Okay, so do we want to work it out so that we each get a fair deal?"), or *haggling* ("Well, it's a pretty expensive lamp, you know, so around maybe $95 seems fair" followed by, "The most I would give for it is $60").

Further, when the negotiation stalled, the friends in the study used two dynamic processes. The first was *trust-testing*. For example, when one pair of friends ran into a problem agreeing on the value of an item they were trying to negotiate, the seller friend built trust with the buyer friend by proposing, "Can we close the range a little bit and maybe we can find a better estimate of where we could moderate the price? When the other responded "Okay," trust was built and the two parties began to reveal more. Another tactic was *process clarification*. For instance, one pair was negotiating over the price of a lamp. The student who was selling communicated her intentions by saying, "You've misinterpreted that; the amount that I paid for the lamp was $39" (because she knew the buyer thought she had only paid $25 originally for the lamp). The other party responded with, "Oh, okay. So, I understand you would have to get more . . ."[52]

A third process tactic, *emotional punctuation*, emerged between strangers, but not between friends. Emotional punctuation is a burst or eruption of strong emotion (e.g., "I'm being very frank with you and I hate people not to be frank with me. . . . At the beginning I was just asking for your price and you were doing all this calculation . . . so I'd rather forego my [profit] than be called a fool!"). Bottom line: emotional punctuation often escalates emotion in the other party, (e.g., "This is definitely a test of greed, isn't it?"), as discussed earlier for anger. Presumably, when we negotiate with friends and loved ones, we put a check on negative emotion, because the stakes involved are so high. But things often get heated with friends and loved ones, too!

Let's face it, the very word "negotiation" conjures images of tough, poker-faced, steely-eyed ruthless characters. And, if word gets out in a community that someone is an "expert in negotiation," well, you can just bet that the gloves will come off. One study by Professor Cathy Tinsley and her colleagues makes this point very clearly.[53] Tinsley found that when amateur negotiators learned that their "opponent" was an "experienced" negotiator, they were much tougher—and collectively reached much lower outcomes—than when the negotiation reputation of the other party was not made public or obvious.

To make this point about negotiation context crystal clear, social scientist Lee Ross did a clever study that involved the Prisoner's Dilemma game.[54] The Prisoner's Dilemma is a highly stylized game that involves two people. Each person must make a choice—without communicating with the opponent—and this decides their fate. You may wonder why it's called that. Well, in the common version of the game, two people are arrested on suspicion that they committed a crime—e.g., robbery—together. However, there's a lack of evidence, so law enforcement officials need a confession from at least one party to implicate both—that is, a confession from either party will result in a guilty verdict for both. Then they present the choices to the protagonists as below, including the jail sentences each player receives in each scenario:

	Partner: Does not confess	Partner: Confesses
You: Do not confess	You: 1 year Partner: 1 year	You: 10 years Partner: Free
You: Confess	You: Free Partner: 10 years	You: 5 years Partner: 5 years

The important point is that you have no control or knowledge of what your partner in crime is going to do. But you have to make a choice in the next five minutes: either confess or don't. It is abundantly clear that the *sweet spot for both of you is not to confess* (i.e., stay mum). In this case, both of you serve little time (one year each) and the situation is as "win-win" as possible. Easy, right? Nope. A large majority of people confess! Why? Well, let's think this through. Suppose you have access to insider knowledge through an informant, and you've learned that your partner plans not to confess. This means you are looking at either a year of jail or going free. Most people would prefer to be free than to go to jail, so they opt to confess (and in so doing, rat on their partner)! Now, suppose that your informant tells you that your partner has actually decided to confess; this means you are facing either ten years or five years of jail time. Most people opt for five years, which requires their confession. Now we have a revelation: we don't need an informant to come to the sobering realization that *no matter what our partner does, it is always better to confess!* Here's the kicker: Your partner is most likely doing the same type of thinking, and if they come to the same conclusion that will mean both of you end up in the lower right (lose-lose) quadrant. This is why it's called the Prisoner's Dilemma: The pursuit of rational and logical outcomes leads to lose-lose. The sweet spot is there, but we often fail to get to it!

So what did Lee Ross find in his study of the game? When the game was called the "Wall Street Game," most people ended up confessing and screwing themselves and their partner. However, when it was called the "Community Game," more people were able to find the sweet spot. The payoffs (i.e., consequences) were the same, but the game's name completely changed people's mindsets. The effect of the word "negotiation" is a lot like "Wall Street"—it brings out competitive, self-interested behavior!

HACK 8 >>>>>>>>>>>>>>>>>>>>>>>>>>>>>>>>>>

Get Your "We" On

Many self-help books encourage people to affirm themselves. For example, a Google search reveals hundreds of titles such as *How to Love Yourself Cards: A Deck of 64 Affirmations* and *Daily Affirmations: 500 Self-Affirmations to Get You Out of Bed in the Morning,* even a coloring book titled, *Color Your Way: A Color Journal + Quotes and Affirmations.* And leading websites like the *Huffington Post* feature affirmation-focused articles that promise to help you, one titled *5 Affirmations That Will Change Your Life.*

Is it possible that there can be too much self-affirmation? Self-affirmation, self-acceptance, and self-focus have put people excessively inside their own heads. Indeed, our research suggests that too much self-focus is a recipe for missing the sweet spot, because it leads us to fail to understand our relational partners. What's more, the more we focus on ourselves, the more likely we are to distort others' views. So our advice is the opposite: Don't affirm yourself, affirm the other. Or, if you do affirm yourself, give equal airtime to affirming the other party.

To test the impact of self- versus other-affirmation on relationship well-being, Tanya Menon and I gave people a list of characteristics and values including: artistic, aesthetic appreciation, sense of humor, relations with friends, spontaneity, and social skills. We asked people to read the list carefully and think about the value that was *least* important to them but *most* important to their relationship partner.[55] We also asked them to write a few sentences on why this value was important to their partner. Then, we asked them how "threatened" they were by the other person and how threatened they believed the other was by them. The people who had affirmed themselves were more likely to believe that they threatened their partner and thus, were more likely to patronize their partner ("He's envious of my success, so I will just minimize my accomplishments"). Conversely, when people affirmed their partner, they did not fall prey to the threat immunity bias, and did not (falsely) believe that they threatened the other party (by virtue of their talents and good looks), and their interactions were more collaborative.

One way of prompting a focus on the other is to stop using "me" words (e.g., "I," "me," "mine," "my," etc.) and use "we" words (e.g., "us," "ours," "we," "both"). One study examined the relationship such personal pronouns (spoken during a marital conversation) have with the emotional tone of marital interactions and with overall marital satisfaction.[56] Specifically, 154 middle-aged and older couples engaged in a fifteen-minute conflict conversation during which the researchers monitored physiological and emotional behavior continuously. Verbatim transcripts of their conversations were coded into two key categories: (a) "we-ness" (we-words), pronouns that focus on the couple; and (b) separateness (me/you-words), pronouns that focus on the individual spouses. More we-ness was associated with a number of desirable qualities, including lower cardiovascular arousal and more positive and less negative emotional behavior; conversely, more "me-ness" was associated with more negative emotional behavior and lower marital satisfaction.

"Liz," a physician friend, shared with me how a "we" conversation was pivotal in her own marriage. She had spent her entire working life as a family physician and had a few kids of her own along the way. She maintained a very small practice and saw mostly elderly patients. Over the years, her malpractice insurance and other costs, like office rent and staff salaries, had risen precipitously. But Liz kept her fees in check—for her beloved patients, many of whom had seen her for over forty years. For years, her husband, George, cajoled Liz, "I wish you would give up your 'hobby' because it is not contributing income!" and "At the rate you're going, neither one of us can ever retire!" But for Liz, treating patients was not about the money; she truly loved taking care of her patients, especially the elderly.

Then Liz received an offer to lead a large-scale health initiative for the elderly (in a different state), that would be a high-impact, but (yet another) low-salaried job, and she considered it seriously. Her husband initially said, "This makes no sense! You're about six years away from retirement and this is not helping us build our nest egg!" Liz paused and said, "We've known each other since medical school. You know that I'm at my best when I'm taking care of the elderly. For me, it's not about the money. Please try to look at this opportunity through my eyes." George understood that he was indeed looking at their careers as related to financial utility maximization alone. When George was challenged to look at Liz's career through a different lens—that of pursuing her "calling"—things started to fall into place. Liz accepted the new position, which she did indeed find to be her calling, and George moved with her, launched a private consulting business, and agreed to delay his own retirement a few more years!

Mirror (Don't Mimic)

Some years ago, several sales organizations became aware of research that essentially showed that when people feel that they are "in sync," they develop greater rapport. One way of developing immediate feelings of rapport is to physically "mirror" another person, which technically means to move your body in similar ways. Consequently, sales personnel were told to "mirror" their customers and clients.

As you might expect, mirroring is a subtle art that takes practice and skill. In this case, some people who attempted to mirror their conversational counterpart, for example, appeared to be mocking or mimicking the other. I talked to a procurement director at a large healthcare organization who told me about a newly minted sales rep he'd interacted with who seemed to have engaged in a crash course on mirroring, which made the rep look foolish. The procurement manager took his business elsewhere.

Does this mean we should throw out the concept of mirroring altogether? Absolutely not. We just need to do it the right way. When we are interacting with someone, we are usually not consciously aware of our nonverbal behavior, with the possible exception of visual eye contact. One of the most important behaviors that paves the way toward trust (and ultimately win-win outcomes) during face-to-face interaction is indeed mirroring, or the reflection of another's body language in our own. This typically happens naturally.

In fact, countless business books prod upwardly mobile managers to engage in "strategic behavioral mimicry" which is the conscious mirroring (sometimes known as mimicking—but not in a mocking sense) of their conversational partner's body language. And guess what? When done right, it appears to work. For example, negotiators who mirror the mannerisms of their opponents secure better negotiated outcomes and are more likely to reach win-win outcomes compared to negotiators who don't consciously mirror.[57] Moreover, timing *does* matter. It's important to start the mirroring process early in the interaction—indeed, people who mirror within the first ten minutes of the interaction are more successful than those who wait until the end. Why? When our conversational partner is behaviorally in sync with us, we feel more trust.

Importantly, when using the mirroring technique in a conflict situation, the key is to mirror *positive* gestures and postures, not *negative* ones. This means that if the other party has their arms crossed and their jaw clenched, it may be unwise to mirror those. Instead, focus on one aspect of the other party's posture or facial expression that is positive, and mirror that. It's important to be subtle and sincere as well.

Mirroring does not just put us in sync with the other party; it has the power to change our attitudes. What I often tell my students and clients is that it is very difficult to change how we *feel* about someone or something; it's actually easier to change our *behavior*. When we modify our behavior, such as with mirroring or using an open body posture, emotions and attitudes may follow.

This is the case because of the *cognitive dissonance effect*, which states that people feel a strong need to bring their attitudes in line with their behaviors, and vice versa.[58] Given that it is often difficult to change our attitude, it is easier to begin with a small behavioral change. I witnessed this firsthand when I was informally coaching Hannah, a young woman in what she described as a "troubled relationship." Hannah explained that she wanted to spend more time with her partner, David, but he didn't seem willing to carve out more leisure time for her. David was putting in long hours at his new position, attempting to make a good impression. Moreover, the small windows of time Hannah and David did have together became increasingly tense, and their conversations seemed to go immediately south.

The cycle needed to be broken. So Hannah decided to try focusing on her behaviors and body language in their next conversation. First, she arranged their meeting spot so she was not sitting directly across from David, which can lead to more of a confrontational interaction, as discussed earlier. When she noticed his defensive, backward-leaning posture, she leaned in and said, "I want to make the most of the short time we have today." Hannah then touched one of his crossed arms and said, "Tell me about your day. What are you learning about this company?" David loosened up and began to recount his day in detail, mentioning that he'd delivered a big achievement. Hannah suggested that a "celebration" might be in order, and they made evening plans. In this way, Hannah used small behavioral changes to begin to melt the ice in her relationship.

A colleague of mine used a behavioral strategy to try to stop a conflict spiral with an aggressive peer. In this case, the peer confronted her in the (public) hallway and raised his voice. Feeling herself being dragged in, my colleague stepped to the side and "imagined his angry words floating over her left shoulder," which helped her maintain her composure. This simple behavioral strategy was much easier for her to employ than trying to "calm down" or "change her attitude."

The relationship hacks we've presented in this chapter call into question some of the common wisdom we've all been exposed to. Much well-meaning relationship advice focuses on minimizing conflict, but when we do so, we're much more likely to cut the orange in half instead of finding the sweet spot. Yet other advice calls for being true to oneself and expressing anger. Neither strategy is particularly helpful.

The next time you find yourself in disagreement with a friend, lover, or neighbor, check the urge to minimize or eliminate the conflict, and also resist the temptation to "let them have a piece of your mind!" Instead, put the focus on them, and think about how you can understand and adopt their perspective. When you feel distrustful, pivot into suspicion. When you feel angry, focus on and express your disappointment. When in doubt, tell your partner that you are committed to finding the sweet spot, and that rather than simply trusting your gut, you want to use principles that have been proven to lead to win-win outcomes.

CHAPTER SIX

Sweet Spot Hacks for the Workplace

MANY PEOPLE HAVE A "SPLIT" PERSONALITY WHEN IT comes to negotiation and conflict—one style they use at the office and a very different style they bring out at home. Sometimes this is their natural style, and in other cases they've cultivated a specific style in one setting over time. Most often it's to fit in with their work culture.

A personality profile we often see is a tough-as-nails versus soft-as-pudding mash-up, such that people are confrontational in the workplace—particularly when the corporate culture encourages toughness, even ruthlessness—but very accommodating at home. Take the case of Wes, a young business manager. When Wes joined his company, the senior leadership group was experimenting with a model of conflict that required people to speak up and disagree with one another without apology—the idea was that blunt confrontation would ultimately be more efficient and reveal optimal, evidence-based solutions. Wes quickly realized that to be taken seriously in his new company, he had to be much more aggressive in the office than he was used to being. Paradoxically, when it came to his personal life, Wes, a self-described "typical middle child," did his best to keep the peace, striving not to rock the boat, with the tolerance of a saint. So Wes had to do his best to bring out a more aggressive version of himself in the office.

We've also seen the opposite pattern: people who are accommodating in the workplace, but overly aggressive at home. For example, Monica described her role in a nonprofit organization where the unstated norm was to be excessively polite, to a fault. After her two decades as a corporate attorney, Monica was not wired for politeness. Even at home, Monica was a proud "tiger mom" (her words), pushing the family to achieve big things and express themselves fully, rather than just keeping the peace. Monica's take-no-prisoners style led to a lot of strife in the nonprofit organization, with coworkers often reminding her, "We are all here because we believe in the mission"—to Monica, that just seemed like a license to underperform.

When the conflict norms of our work environment are nearly the polar opposite of those of our home, it requires toggling between two extremes: *tough-as-nails* and *soft-as-pudding*. This behavioral swing is not easy, as the examples of Wes and Monica suggest. Moreover, neither conflict style is particularly effective.

In this book, we encourage people to have a consistent conflict style at home and at work that can pave the way toward mutually profitable, highly rewarding sweet spot solutions. However, people often have a hard time envisioning what such a win-win conflict style might look like. That's because many of us hold faulty beliefs about conflict—beliefs perpetuated by stories, myths, TV, and other media, which all tend to focus on extremes. These beliefs can hold us back from finding the sweet spot in our business and personal relationships. So it's worth exposing the faulty beliefs, to help us recognize them and put them to rest. The sections below explore faulty beliefs while providing tips for effective negotiation.

Fight or Flight?

The two most common conflict styles are the tough-as-nails and soft-as-pudding types discussed above. The aggressive, tough-as-nails negotiator charges into the boxing ring ready to fight. The passive, soft-as-pudding negotiator melts in the face of conflict, often seeking an easy exit by capitulating. The problem is that many people falsely believe they must choose between super-tough or super-soft. But that leads to poor outcomes because neither style is ideal: The tough-as-nails negotiator often leaves a path of resentment in their wake and usually starts a costly, escalating spiral of conflict; the soft-as-pudding accommodator makes relational sacrifices and ends up down the road in Abilene (an example of group capitulation presented in Chapter Five) or at their least preferred vacation spot.

So, you ask, what's the solution? Should we aim for a nice midpoint between the warmonger and the creampuff? Certainly not, because a middle-of-the-road style inevitably results in an orange split down the middle. The effective negotiator needs to do two things. First and foremost, figure out the shared goals in the situation—what aligns us? Second, determine where the differences are and how to leverage them. Thus, the most effective style is to highlight the differences— even magnify them—with the goal of leveraging them.

Too often, we see people who are blind to the shared goals. The tough-as-nails negotiator does not see the shared goals: "We're in complete disagreement" they believe, or "We're not on the same page." The creampuff, in contrast, is not willing to acknowledge any differences in the first place. Overly focused on finding the areas of agreement, they end up with no differences to leverage. In this sense, just like our old friends the sisters, who never realized that one wanted the juice and the other the peel, both groups miss valuable opportunities.

The moral, then, is not to aim for an extreme position or middle-of-the-road one, but one that enables you to identify and leverage differences effectively. For example, when Facebook CEO Mark Zuckerberg offered Google VP Sheryl Sandberg a fantastically lucrative offer to join Facebook as their new COO, Sheryl nearly took the offer on the spot.[1] But she stopped herself and, in their next conversation, leveraged their interests by explaining, "This is the only time you and I will ever be on opposite sides of the table," making the point that she would be negotiating huge deals for Facebook and training the Facebook negotiation team. Next, she proceeded to lay out what she wanted from the role/deal. "So where's the orange?" you may ask. Zuckerberg needed a no-nonsense COO like Sandberg to deal with everyone from the Justice Department to acquisition targets, along with training internal people; and Sheryl wanted to negotiate a deal that she would be proud of for years to come. They both got what they wanted because Sandberg encouraged leveraging differences.[2]

Win-Win Hacks for the Workplace

Negotiation at work often involves collaborating with colleagues and coworkers (internal negotiations) and with outside parties, such as customers, clients, suppliers, vendors, and acquisition targets (external negotiations). Most people regard external negotiations to be both more combative and easier than negotiating with colleagues, because there often exists a script, mechanism, or protocol to conduct external negotiations. Moreover, there is less risk of retribution or payback, precisely because those in negotiation don't work together. But it's important to understand the exact nature of each negotiation situation to approach it effectively.

For example, Jay is a commercial space designer who gets most of his contracts by responding to RFPs (requests for proposals). The RFP process is, on the surface, extremely competitive, as a company is essentially pitting several bidders against one another and will choose only one. In one instance, Jay submitted a bid to a property developer, along with several other designers. When I interviewed Jay, I asked, "Do you think that the developer is trying to turn this RFP into a price war where the lowest bidder will win?" Jay said, "No. The property developer does not want to start a bidding war over price because they care about quality and innovation." Thus, Jay looks at the entire process not as a strict competition but as a creative challenge. In fact, in this case the property developer invited four different design companies—Jay's included—to submit a design for a fixed price. The developer wanted to see what each design company could do for a given price. Thus, the competition was about innovation, rather than price, as Jay suggested.

Now, to be sure, many RFPs are based nearly exclusively on price, and they do incentivize bidders to compete against one another. This essentially amounts to a fixed-sum situation. However, in most RFPs it's the case that there are pivotal issues besides "price"—such as timeline, scope of work, and so on. By recognizing these other factors, it is often possible to find a sweet spot solution, rather than taking a price-is-everything approach.

Scripted versus Unscripted

Jay's RFP above is an example of a "scripted" negotiation. So is buying a car or selling a house, which are also scripted negotiations, meaning they involve norms, roles, protocols, and forms. The script provides a mechanism by which parties can conduct the negotiation without apologizing for being "tough."

However, many internal conflicts, or those that take place among coworkers, typically do not come with a script. A conflict at work that escalates into angry threats may lead to years of bitter feelings, creating a toxic workplace for everyone involved. For example, in one large organization, a feud occurred between two people that was particularly emotional and bitter. At the heart of it was the question of project ownership—who ultimately deserved credit for a major contribution. In this case, the disputants attempted to build coalitions by coaxing other members of their department to take sides. Soon, battle lines were drawn and colleagues found it difficult to be neutral or uninvolved, as every action seemed to benefit a particular disputant. After a lengthy period, the conflict was resolved through a professional mediator and, ultimately, one of the protagonists left the organization. However, the bitter feelings from the battle affected the organization's climate long after.

When we don't have a script, as is the case in many internal negotiations, disputants may have wildly different ideas about what is appropriate to do (or not to do). Moreover, they cannot easily walk away from the table because they are in a long-term relationship, meaning there is "history" and the expectation of future interaction. Moreover, the social and reputational stakes are much higher when it involves colleagues. Bottom line: The lack of a script and the relational stakes make negotiating with coworkers particularly risky.

What we often find is that in the absence of a script, people in the workplace do one of two things: they adopt the tough-as-nails style or play it safe and take the soft-as-pudding approach. Neither of these strategies is effective, as noted earlier.

Most business books on negotiation have focused on external negotiations—such as vendor and customer or procurement and sales. Indeed, most of the managers and executives that I work with feel much more comfortable negotiating outside the company than within its walls. So, we need a hack for workplace negotiations—the situations that pop up routinely at work that don't come with a script, protocol, or bidding mechanism but have a profound impact on our quality of life.

Here are thirteen hacks for negotiation in the workplace.

HACK 10 >>>

Agree on the Process (Before Getting into the Substance)

On one occasion, I was working with an international professional services firm that had the goal of encouraging more alignment and sharing of best practices across geographies and lines of business. Everyone worked at the same company, but each office essentially operated as its own profit center, so there were few incentives for sharing business. I got interested in the relationship between two groups in the company, call them X and Y. There was a great deal of "history" between the X and

Y groups, as they represented different divisions and geographies; yet several factors, including regulatory changes and supplier relationships, had thrust them together. The question was: Could they put down their battle swords and attempt to collaborate? To make matters even trickier, two top division leaders also had "history"—and both of them were alpha-types who were used to controlling the situation.

As part of a corporate training event, I arranged for a role-play simulation that was hauntingly similar to the inter-division situation in their company (involving two different business units within a single firm). In both the simulation and real life, to be effective in a competitive landscape would require them to get past their acrimonious history. To prepare, I divided the managers into teams (that reflected their actual work relationships) and gave each team a briefing sheet and a fixed time to "negotiate"—in this case, about seventy-five minutes. I assigned each pair of teams a private room where they could meet, with the expectation that at the end of seventy-five minutes they would ideally agree on some terms. Of course, the scenario I used had a hidden sweet spot (like most such simulations), but it was not obvious to the business managers, at least on the surface.

As the seventy-five-minute window was closing, several groups were huddled in the hallway, arms crossed—a typical, eleventh-hour negotiation. One group, however, was nowhere in sight. Good heavens, I thought, where are they? At exactly one minute before the deadline the group "missing in action" returned with a typed proposal that they thrust into the hands of the opposing team, solemnly and definitively announcing, "Take it or leave it."

Their strategy, it turned out, had been not to engage in any dialogue at all with the opposing business unit and simply to deliver a last-minute ultimatum; it all resembled a game of "chicken."[3] Knowing that the consequences of failing to reach a deal were uniformly calamitous for both groups, the receiving group begrudgingly agreed to the ultimatum (presumably to prevent all parties from driving off the cliff). However, they publicly vowed to "never forget this and seek future retribution."

What's the takeaway? In the absence of a negotiation process or script, people often avoid negotiation, go into combat mode, or otherwise insult the other party. In the situation described above, the business leaders did not have a script, took their cues from their past (acrimonious) history, feared the worst, and defaulted into game-playing mode. "What should we have done, Professor?" asked the disgruntled receiving team. "Those guys just disappeared and we were stuck here for seventy-five minutes waiting for them to show up!"

When workplace conflict situations go sour and completely unravel, it's not necessarily because the parties disagree about the substantive issues. It's because they unknowingly insult one another through their actions and behaviors: "I don't like the way they are talking to us"; "How dare they think they can walk in and start dictating!"; and "Did you see the way they rolled their eyes?" Unfortunately, these negotiations often end before they even formally begin. We need a hack!

The solution is to agree on a *process* before getting into the *substance* of the negotiation.

Negotiators may not agree on the substance, but if they can agree on a process, that's a good start. Let me give you an example of a negotiation in which one of the parties—an obviously seasoned professional who had no doubt experienced some process meltdowns in past negotiations—beautifully initiated a complex, internal, multiparty negotiation by focusing on the process before getting into the substance:

"Look, this is a complex business matter for all of us. There is a lot of strong feeling and emotion about this matter because at the present time, we are not on the same page. Before we get into the issues, I'm wondering if we can spend ten minutes talking about how to best use our mutual time together? For the first ten minutes, let's set aside the business and financial issues and just figure out how best to think about having this conversation in the next week. If there are any ground rules or norms we might want to use, I'm completely open. In the end, our goal is to resolve this and move forward."

The opposing team let out a collective sigh of relief and, for the next ten minutes, the groups discussed how to use their time together when they actually began the formal meeting. Several times, the other team started to explain their position and get into the business issues. As facilitator, I was careful to intervene in such instances, gently reminding them that by their own agreement this was a "process discussion" only. Then, the manager who had suggested the process discussion floated several specific process options: "We can jointly brainstorm a list of the issues (to discuss later), or we can each create independent lists of the issues that we can share." The other team said, "Can we make a list of things that are off the table?" "Sure" said the other team leader, adding, "But let's agree that for now we are only making suggestions, and not indicating whether we agree or disagree with a given suggestion." In the end, the group spent thirty minutes talking about how their next meeting could proceed, created several homework assignments, and agreed on a time and place to meet. One party added that he would like everyone to agree not to involve others outside the room or to send emails to anyone prior to that meeting. Everyone agreed.

When it came time for the actual business negotiation the next week, the mood was very amicable, collective trust was high, the group felt relaxed, and the result was an extremely constructive discussion that, in fact, led to a sweet spot agreement. The reason this happened is that the process had been discussed and agreed upon ahead of time. Both parties were co-owners of the process, which smoothed their way to finding the sweet spot.

HACK 11 >>>>>>>>>>>>>>>>>>>>>>>>>>>>>>>>

Lose the Poker Face

"Keep a poker face."[4]

Virtually everyone in the business world has been admonished to reveal as little as possible to the opposing party. This essentially amounts to keeping a "poker face" by not revealing your interests, pain points, true goals, and emotions. The belief is that if these are exposed, the opponent can and will take advantage of you. Keeping a poker face prevents that, the wisdom goes.

As a negotiation researcher, I kept hearing this advice from the seasoned business people I interviewed. During my dissertation days, for example, I asked several executives about what information they should *reveal* versus *conceal* in business negotiations. "Don't reveal anything," most of them plainly said. One even shook his head, and said, "Haven't you ever heard the expression 'keep a poker face'?"

I kept wondering exactly how things would play out if two people who both believed in the poker face strategy were seated across the negotiating table from each other. Who would speak first? Would anybody say anything? Fortunately, I had opportunities to witness and hear about how many of these poker-faced negotiations played out in mysterious and sometimes downright comical ways.

For example, an executive student in my class recounted a complex negotiation involving a project budget. The other party was a colleague in his organization who had her own set of priorities for the project. They disagreed about headcounts and timing. This was a matrix organization that had complex reporting relationships, different functions, and different geographies.

Because there were multiple issues on the table, we suspected that there could be a win-win opportunity lurking below the surface, but it might not have been obvious because both parties were closely guarding their information, value drivers, and pain points. Each wanted the other party to show their hand first. However, both parties came from the poker face school of thought. This led to a comical situation in which both parties seated at the table tried to bait the other into revealing something first. Neither wanted to be taken in by the other, so the conversation became increasingly odd, often rambling into topics completely outside the scope of the situation: "So, how are you liking the new CEO?" one party said. "Well enough," the other replied. "Have you guys recovered from the big reorg?"—with both straining to maintain rigid poker faces. This negotiation was ultimately never consummated, and the regional VP had to intervene. To be sure, this did not result in the best outcome for the parties involved, a direct result of the misguided poker face strategy!

I became so preoccupied with this "You go first" paradox that in my dissertation I included a study where I essentially forced people to tip their hand because I wanted to know whether revealing information did, in fact, put a negotiator in a position of weakness.[5] Once again, I used a business case scenario in which two businesspeople appeared to have diametrically opposing interests regarding a business transaction—price, volume, quantity, services, etc.—but the situation actually contained potential for a truly profitable win-win deal, or a sweet spot. I was also careful to measure people's fixed-pie perceptions at several points during the actual negotiation.

But I included a twist. I randomly told one of the players to reveal two pieces of information in the first five minutes of the negotiation: namely, their rank-ordering of the business issues involved and their most desired set of terms for those issues. I recorded the interactions (with their permission!) to see whether the "revealer" would then be "played" (i.e., taken advantage of by the counterparty).

The results? Not only was the revealer *not* taken advantage of, but both of the negotiators created better deals (i.e., more sweet spot agreements) than the control group! In the control group condition, I simply told the businesspeople to negotiate and do and say anything they wanted. Only about 7 percent of them asked value-finding questions! Most of the time, they simply made demands. Bottom line: People who revealed important information about their value drivers and rank-ordering of the issues created more sweet spot deals than those left to their own devices.

I then experimented with a condition in which some people "questioned" the counterparty (e.g., "What's most important to you?") and, again, found that these negotiators created dramatically better deals than the control group. Try as I might, I have not found evidence that revealing value drivers or pain points puts a negotiator at risk. So it's really about using an "I go first" strategy!

What's more, the simple question "What's important to you?" is a great conversation starter. It's not a power move; it's a *relationship* move. Music agent Troy Carter was virtually bankrupt before he gained the client of his career: Lady Gaga (famous for the song "Poker Face," coincidentally). His key to success is his ability to form relationships and "read the room" (a.k.a. perspective-taking) to figure out exactly what the parties in question want. When Carter first encountered Stefani Germanotta, also known as Lady Gaga, she was an unknown artist who had just been dropped by Def Jam Records. Carter himself had recently lost his biggest client, Eve Jeffers. So both he and Germanotta were down-and-out. Upon meeting Gaga and hearing her music, Carter was intrigued because Germanotta expressed her desire to "change the game [music]." This gave Carter an idea. Both of them had fallen into the crevasse of the music industry. So, Carter figured out a way to sidestep the traditional model and avoid the power-holders of traditional record labels: He poured his energy into booking gigs for Gaga at gay clubs and fashion events, and used social media apps including Twitter, Facebook, and YouTube to enable Gaga's fans to find and share her music online, further bypassing typical music distribution methods. It was through the process of mutual revelation of heartfelt interests that Carter and Gaga found their incredibly lucrative orange. Under Carter's guidance, Gaga went from performance artist, to pop star, to a global brand, which was exactly what she said she wanted.[6]

By now, it's probably more than clear that in order to find the "win-win" potential, more than one issue (or point of contention) needs to be at stake. If the negotiation is simply about a one-time cash price, then we have a fixed-sum situation. Unfortunately, many of life's negotiations appear to be just about *price*—buying a house, buying a car, negotiating a salary. Even our old friends the sisters (falsely) believed that their negotiation was about a single orange, leading to their misguided even-Steven split.

But what about the real world, where most people are not haggling about oranges, but about price? The seller wants a high price; the buyer wants a low one. And there they are. So, what to do? Answer: Find or add another issue. For example, if the method of payment, or terms of payment are also negotiable, then we can most likely convert this fixed-sum situation into a win-win.

Here's an example. When Delta Air Lines negotiated a $5.6 billion deal with Canadian aircraft-maker Bombardier to purchase seventy-five CS100 airliners, this was a win-win for both Delta and Bombardier.[7] Why? Delta had been struggling with their aging fleet of aircraft, while Bombardier had suffered significant development delays. The key to this win-win negotiation was both price and timing. Because Delta had one of the oldest fleets in the industry, they saw an opportunity to upgrade their aircraft at a substantial discount. In return, Bombardier gained a big customer who agreed to close the deal soon, allowing them to make up for past delays and send a signal to other potential customers that their development problems were behind them.

Another example: when National Hockey League owners and players were embroiled in a crippling 112-day lockout in 2012–2013, the main point of contention was the construction of a new ten-year collective bargaining agreement between the players' union and league owners. Midway through challenging negotiations, a new issue was introduced—namely, limits on how much less in salary a veteran player could make from one year to the next. Both parties were then able to make concessions and began playing hockey once again.[8] All of these examples make clear how being willing to offer something—key issues, preferences, new terms—leads to better outcomes than playing things with a poker face.

HACK 12 >>>>>>>>>>>>>>>>>>>>>>>>>>>>>>>>>>>

Dessert Tray

Sometimes, businesspeople get stuck. They've divided the negotiation orange into multiple meaningful slices and prioritized the issues, but still seem to be going in circles. They need something to jumpstart the negotiation and, further, an effective way to find a sweet spot deal, if it exists. So is there a strategy they can use in this situation?

Yes! The "dessert tray" method is a personal favorite, probably because I've used it so many times and it has always broken even the toughest deadlock. Let me explain by using a very specific situation that Troy, one of my students, found himself in. As director of sales and operations for his company, Troy negotiated deals on charter flights for customer groups. In this specific instance, Troy was dealing with a very important customer: a large organization representing several collegiate athletic programs. So he was concerned about retaining their business.

There were several issues under negotiation, including price discounts, aircraft type, schedule, and party size. Unfortunately, the customer was taking a hard line on all of them, at one point even threatening to look for "some other bids!" Well, that was the last thing Troy wanted, because he couldn't afford to enter a bidding war with competitors. The key, then, was for Troy to try to figure out what the customer's most important priorities were across the different issues. Enter the dessert tray hack, which helps you figure out the other party's value drivers when they're not willing to volunteer them!

The key to the dessert tray hack is to find as many issues of value—moving parts—as possible. Troy used the brainstorming technique to identify five key key issues in addition to price: aircraft type, schedule, size of party, amenities, and future bookings. Next, Troy created several combinations of these issues that were all of *equal desirability* to him. That's the secret to the dessert tray method: you have to create combinations that you see as equally valuable. Troy referred to the different combinations as Options A, B, C, and so on, then presented them to the customer and asked him to rank-order them from best to worst. Troy was careful not to ask the customer whether these options were "acceptable"—rather, he just asked for the ranking. Very quickly, Troy gained valuable insights about the tough customer's actual value drivers when the customer ranked two of the options as best. So Troy knew that those specific combinations represented the sweet spot better than the others.

Next, Troy studied the customer's preferred options and was able to make very good guesses about the issues the customer cared most about—specifically, schedule and size of party. So, even though the customer was not communicating directly about his largest priorities, the dessert tray hack allowed Troy to deduce these preferences through reverse-engineering.

Ultimately, by using the dessert tray method Troy successfully avoided being dragged into a bidding war with other competitors and crafted a deal that was not only the best for the customer but of great value to his own company—a sweet spot deal!

HACK 13 >>>>>>>>>>>>>>>>>>>>>>>>>>>>>>>>>>>

Columbo Method

My parent's favorite TV show was *Columbo*. For those of you who managed to miss this show (or were not born yet!), it starred actor Peter Falk as a bumbling but annoyingly persistent police lieutenant. He would come face-to-face with the suspected murderer, ask a series of questions the perpetrator seemed to answer well enough, and then, as he was walking away, Columbo would stop, turn around, and say, "Oh, just one more thing . . . ." (or sometimes, "I've got just one more question . . ."). This would frustrate the suspect, who thought he was about to get away with murder; slowly but surely, Lieutenant Columbo would "close in," and eventually back the suspect into a corner. Okay, so now you're probably wondering how on earth this "Just one more question" method applies to win-win negotiation.

Let me explain by using my own executive class as an example. In one session, I gave my students an hour to negotiate a complex, multi-issue deal. Most of them were able to reach a mutual agreement, but when I looked at their performance, they hadn't optimized. Only one team had reached the sweet spot; the great majority had settled for the low-hanging fruit. They thought they were headed for a coffee break and then I turned and said, "Oh, just one more thing . . . we're actually not going on break right now." They were annoyed—just like the murder suspects on *Columbo*. Then I said, "I want everyone to go back to your negotiation tables and see if you can come up with a deal that both of you like more than the one you have already agreed to." This directive raised even more confusion: "Hey, Prof, is this a renegotiation? A do-over?" "No," I explained, "you each already have a deal that is valid. Now, I want to see whether you can mutually improve upon it. If you can't, then you live with the current deal."

At first, most were confused: "We have a deal already. Why would we change it?" I replied, "Just humor me!" They reluctantly went back to their meeting rooms, sat back in their chairs, and started to explore. Within thirty minutes, *every group* had reached a new set of terms that was better for all parties! The one group that had already optimized apologetically told me that the exercise was a "waste of time" and said they were going on a coffee break now no matter what!

What I call the Columbo Method is a strategy that goes by the formal name of *post-settlement settlement*.[9] The idea is that once negotiators reach a deal, they should attempt to mutually improve upon it. However, the key element is that *neither party has veto power*. This method essentially incentivizes both parties to care about the other's interests because the only way that Party A can improve is to help Party B, and vice-versa.

A really nice example of an after-the-deal deal is one that "Mike," a former student executive of mine, did when he was buying a New Jersey-based company from an entrepreneur. Mike reached a deal with the entrepreneur that was formally signed. Yet during the entire negotiation, Mike noticed that the entrepreneur was very hesitant despite the fact that every spreadsheet showed that the entrepreneur would make more money by selling (than by not selling) to Mike. This told Mike that the hesitation was not about the money. Over a post-negotiation coffee, the entrepreneur sighed and said, "Now I've got to figure out how to tell the guy in Miami that he doesn't have a job anymore." The reason the "Miami guy" did not have a job anymore was because one of Mike's stipulations was a strict "no remote worker" policy. So Mike tested the waters: "What if I transferred the clients that I don't need or want to your Miami-based project manager?" The entrepreneur was thrilled because this would mean that the entrepreneur would be giving the Miami guy a full book of new business instead of a pink slip! It got even better when the entrepreneur reduced his asking price because Mike would not be getting revenue from these (unwanted) clients. In the end, this was a real sweet spot deal because the entrepreneur felt like he did right by his friend/employee in a location that Mike (the buyer) had no interest in. They drew up a new formal contract that they both liked much more than the first one!

In case you are wondering whether the Columbo method works because of the additional amount of *time* people are given to craft deals, the answer is no. How do we know this? We did a simple study in which we gave some people one hour to negotiate, another group two hours, and a third group one hour plus 30 minutes of post-settlement opportunity. There were no appreciable differences between the one- and two-hour groups—both of them had largely satisfied. However, the group who segmented the negotiation into two parts: deal #1 and then improve-upon-deal #1, crafted deals that were a sea-change better than those of everyone else. A great majority of them found the sweet spot or came very close to it. Hack truth: It's not how much time you have to negotiate, it's how you use your time.

HACK 14 >>>>>>>>>>>>>>>>>>>>>>>>>>>>>>>>>>

Skin in the Game

Negotiations often get stalemated and stall out because parties cannot agree about certain events or situations. They steadfastly hold to their own views of the world and attempt to educate and enlighten their colleagues (or spouses): "Here's why I'm right!" However, this persuasion technique usually only makes the target of the persuasion more entrenched in their views. Disagreement morphs into distrust and even contempt. Is there a way out of the quicksand?

Yes! My favorite strategy is what I call the *skin in the game* method. I think this is because I like a good wager and it's also because I'm kind of pigheaded. Let me use my own past situation to explain how it works. In this case, I was negotiating with one of my clients about a training session. I had a long-term relationship with him, and wanted to keep it that way. But the client was pressuring me to give him a steep price reduction—less than half of what I would quote to other clients. This presented a problem for me. My client was using our long-term relationship as a bargaining tool: "Hey, look at how long we've known each other," he pleaded. He promised the lower price would lead to more business in the future. Frankly I was not so sure this would happen, not least of which because of some budget cuts I knew were going on at his company. We both presented our arguments, all the while trying to be diplomatic in saying, "I think you are wrong." The fact is, I was convinced that my dimmer view of the future was accurate and he was convinced his brighter one was. So, what to do, given that we had no access to a time machine?

The skin in the game hack was our solution. Here's how it worked. We set up a simple contingency term that stated that I would give him a (deep) price discount on the current training session, provided that another group in his company scheduled a training session within six months. If that did not happen, then he would pay the full price. Each of us walked away from the table feeling that we had won—that means we'd found the sweet spot. Now, in fact, only one of us would be "right," but the important part is that we were able to leverage our different beliefs. As it turned out, I "won" the bet because there was no other client group who scheduled a session within the six-month period. Now look, even though I "won" the bet, if I had not, I would have still have been satisfied (thrilled, even) with the outcome. That's a key benefit of hitting the sweet spot.

HACK 15 >>

Write on the Walls

As I walked down the hall in my executive center last spring, I saw a red-faced man on his phone. I recognized him as a student in one of my classes (let's call him Abe). It was obvious things weren't going well. "I'll be late to class," he said, rolling his eyes and pointing to his phone. "My business partner is driving me crazy with this buyout deal."

Abe came back to class after the first break and shared some of the (gory) details with me: Abe was trying to extricate himself from a soured business partnership and, in his words, the business partner was being "unreasonable" and even threatening to involve (expensive) lawyers.

Even though Abe might have been looking for sympathy or someone to commiserate with, I immediately put on my negotiation hat. I asked him, "What are your interests? What do you care about in this buyout?"

I walked over to the classroom's large chalkboard with Abe and drew three columns. The first column was everything that was at stake—both economic and intangible. Abe listed several financial concerns, along with his professional reputation, personal time, and stress level. In the second column, I asked Abe to wave a wand and indicate what would be the best possible outcome for each of those at-stake concerns. I also asked him to look down the entire list and rank-order his concerns from "most important" to "moderately important" to "less important," using a simple 1 to 5 scale. The third column was for Abe's business partner. "Oh, this guy, he's an 'xxx-hole,'" Abe said. "Okay," I said, "let's set that aside for a moment. Look," I said, "if xxx-hole was here, tell me what he would say to me about *what* he wants and *why* he wants it." Then I had Abe make his best guess about xxx-hole's rank-ordering. I also asked Abe if there would be other factors or issues that his business partner might want to add to the first column (if he had been with us), and he listed some.

After thirty minutes of shoulder-to-shoulder work, we created a positions-and-interests chart that listed the key issues involved—in this case, the cash buyout, current employees, existing equipment and technology, building rental, professional reputation, time, stress, and so on. And we acknowledged that Abe might not have included all the issues. We also realized that some of the issues appeared to be more important to Abe than to xxx-hole, at least by Abe's estimation.

The next day, Abe came into class early . . . with a big smile on his face. He had just gotten off the phone with his "angry" business partner (xxx-hole was now called "Simon"). Abe had shared the positions-and-interests chart with Simon. Abe had asked Simon to correct his understanding of the issues, add and subtract issues, and comment on his rank-ordering. Abe had also told Simon that he was not attempting to "negotiate" at all, but rather just to get whatever facts and opinions that Simon might have. By lunch, the two of them had reached a preliminary deal.

HACK 16 >>>>>>>>>>>>>>>>>>>>>>>>>>>>>>>>>>>>

Lawyer "Down"

On one occasion, I was negotiating with a large client company about a complex contract agreement. I am no contract attorney, and my eyes were red from trying make sense of the twenty-seven-page "boilerplate" contract that their procurement people had sent me the day prior. A colleague suggested that I retain an attorney to make sure I wasn't going to be "screwed" in the process. So, I retained an attorney, who then marked up the contract and drafted a strongly worded email for me to send to the company, outlining my concerns and requests. My gut instinct was, "Wow, this language does not sound like me." But I sent the email off anyway.

In retrospect I wish I had followed my instinct not to. Very soon, I found out the hard way that my language obviously didn't sound like me in the eyes of the large company either, because of their response. After I sent the email and the red-lined contract, there were three days of radio silence. On the fourth morning, a lengthy, formal email (with several cc's) appeared in my inbox from the company—with more tough language and even threats. Good lord, I thought, what have I done? The genie was out of the bottle! It was clear that the company had involved their own attorneys, and the situation was quickly becoming more litigious. My failure? I hadn't followed my gut instinct—which was simply to call my client company to talk, or to ask for a sit-down with my contact there, rather than "lawyering up," as they say.

At that point, I decided to follow my gut—better late than never—and attempted a mid-course correction. I called my contact at the company and said I thought it might be a good idea to press the reset button, set aside the contract, and engage in a clarifying conversation. I suggested that we see whether we could reach an agreement "in principle"—with the clear understanding that nothing was legally binding until both parties agreed in writing. It took three or four phone calls, but we eventually got there. Through nonbinding conversation, we were able to agree on terms. The conversation allowed us both to brainstorm without fear that we would be held to the written terms.

This experience points to the difference between *legal* contracts and *psychological* contracts. A legal contract is a formal document enforceable in a court of law, and usually contains a lot of (scary) language that requires legal professionals to interpret. A psychological contract (also known as a "handshake" deal) is an understanding reached between people based on trust and goodwill.[10] Whereas psychological contracts may not be as enforceable in court as a legal contract, the parties involved usually treat these like legal contracts. And that's why a psychological contract is so powerful as a negotiation tool. So always think about whether it makes sense to "lawyer down" and go with a psychological contract over a legal one.

This can work even on the largest scales. Some time ago, when I read about the unique multimillion-dollar negotiation deal between Taco Bell and Frito Lay, I thought back to my negotiation with the large company procurement team. Considered by many to be the most successful product launch in Taco Bell history, the Doritos Locos Taco (DLT) netted more than $450 million in sales, representing a 14 percent sales jump from the previous year.[11] Here's the interesting part: When the CEOs of Doritos and Taco Bell met, they did not involve attorneys and did not write a contract at all. They did a handshake-only deal and agreed that if either of them got sacked or promoted, only then would they bother to write a contract.[12] A multimillion-dollar handshake deal!

Several more examples of handshake agreements exist in multimillion-dollar business deals. For example, when Disney chief Bob Iger and 21st Century Fox chairman Rupert Murdoch explored a merger deal, they did it one-on-one over meals and wine.[13] No PowerPoints, no formal offers, and no attorneys. For two months, Iger and Murdoch met only in private, leaving attorneys and meddlesome senior executives at both companies strategically out of the loop. Two months later, Iger and Murdoch stood arm-in-arm atop a London skyscraper to announce their proposed deal. In May of 2019, the deal was finalized, with Disney purchasing much of Rupert Murdoch's Fox for $71.3 billion.[14]

HACK 17 >>>>>>>>>>>>>>>>>>>>>>>>>>>>>>>>>>>>>>

Brainwriting

I've spent over a decade studying brainstorming and helping companies and organizations hold successful brainstorming sessions. Brain*writing* is a variation on brainstorming that is even more effective. So, what's the difference? Brainstorming is when a group generates *oral* ideas; brainwriting is the generation of *written* ideas in a group. In a typical brainstorming session, people are supposed to generate ideas without regard to feasibility or quality—the idea being that even absurd or impractical ideas might act as a catalyst for an ultimately viable idea. Sounds good, right? The problem is that in brainstorming sessions, only one person can speak at any given moment, and others usually have to listen, which may result in their losing their train of thought. Even worse, they may feel that they need to conform to others' ideas or feel intimidated about presenting their own.

Brainwriting, then, is an elegant brainstorming hack. It involves three steps: First, people in a group individually generate written ideas (as many as they want). Second, the full set of written ideas are posted for all to see, but no idea owners are revealed. Moreover, no one can attempt to guess who said what. Third, each person in the group votes on the ideas that they find most promising and intriguing. The group can repeat this process several times. So, how might brainwriting be implemented to resolve workplace conflict? As a case in point, Tess, a manager in my class, confessed to me that she was very frustrated because the people on her research team—all PhD scientists—constantly bickered and undermined her weekly staff meetings. Tess was being run ragged attempting to get the scientists aligned on research priorities and deliverables. So I worked with her to implement a three-step brainwriting intervention. At the next weekly meeting, Tess came with a briefcase filled with hundreds of blank 3" x 5" index cards. As a first step, Tess asked all the scientists to write down their priorities for the research team. She encouraged the scientists to use as many cards as they needed, and to propose multiple goals. Tess was careful to institute two rules: "no guessing" and "no confessions," which meant that no one should sign their name on a card or guess idea owners once the cards were posted.

As a second step, Tess posted the cards on the conference-room wall with thumbtacks and asked all members to read the cards. It turns out some of the cards were highly similar; so Tess grouped these together. As a third step, Tess gave each of the team members five Post-it notes with the instructions to "vote for your top five priorities to discuss and elaborate further on." Within a few minutes, there was consensus around a half dozen priorities.

Tess then asked small teams to take each of the high-priority initiatives and develop them further on a flipchart. She gave each group only about fifteen minutes; afterward, others could provide feedback via more Post-it notes.

Tess kept rotating between private ideation (index cards), group ideation (flipcharts), and feedback (Post-its). In a short time, the team had reached consensus on their research goals. And the subsequent meetings were much more productive. The brainwriting approach had solved Tess's problem.

One type of negotiation-specific brainstorming is a *devising seminar*. A devising seminar is an off-the-record, facilitated workshop in which key stakeholders in negotiations brainstorm mutually advantageous approaches to their conflict challenges.[15] Devising seminars include both unofficial and official stakeholders; they bring people together in their personal rather than their official capacities. Just like brainstorming, devising seminars don't attempt to produce binding agreements, rather, the focus is on generating ideas. As with brainwriting, this is done by emphasizing anonymity of ideas. Interviewers ask stakeholder representatives to share their interests, and all the findings are recorded in an assessment report with responses anonymized.

Anonymous Tip

One of my favorite social science experiments looked at how people reacted to proposed solutions in a conflict situation. The conflict situation in question was particularly tense because it involved "traditionalist" educators in disagreement with "revisionist" educators in California school districts. The conflict centered upon what books should form the core of the English curriculum. Not surprisingly, the traditionalists preferred the classics—e.g., *Macbeth*, *The Iliad*, *Paradise Lost*, etc. The revisionists preferred a different set of books, that involved more diverse viewpoints: *Mrs. Dalloway*, *The Woman Warrior*, *Native Son*, etc.

This was a highly contentious debate fueled by strong emotion. Moreover, the conflict took place in the public arena. Researchers Robert Robinson and Dacher Keltner wondered if the disputants were exaggerating the views of the opposing party, thereby blinding them to a sweet spot solution.[16] So, they asked each of the groups to generate two lists: One list was the books they desired to see on the English curriculum; the other list was the books they believed the *opposing side* wanted. Thus each group (i.e., traditionalists and revisionists) was asked to *predict* what books the opposing party would want on the school curriculum. Then they looked at the two lists to see if there was any overlap. Not surprisingly, the opposing camps assumed that they would have *no* choices in common, when in actual fact the parties shared *seven* books in common, dramat-

127

ically more than they realized. This study reveals an important insight about workplace conflict—namely, the exaggeration of disagreement.

This is a sobering example of how parties embroiled in conflict often have faulty, exaggerated perceptions of the opposing party's interests. In conflict and negotiation, most people believe that they are in more disagreement than they actually are. Moreover, people are often quick to dismiss suggestions offered by the opposing side: "If they want it, then it can't be good for us," goes the thinking. This tendency to immediately dismiss the opponent's ideas ("No way, that's not in my interest") and to magnify actual conflict is known as *reactive devaluation*.[17] Think of reactive devaluation as a knee-jerk response wherein people on opposite sides of the aisle reject one another before they've even heard their ideas (e.g., "Whatever you're offering, I don't want it!").

So how can we hack this? The hack, similar to brainwriting discussed in Hack #17, is to remove the alleged author. For example, when the author of the idea is changed to make it appear that idea was proposed by a member of *one's own party*, people are much more receptive to it! The key takeaway is that people often dismiss and derogate ideas based merely on the source of the proposal versus its actual content. This is why effective mediators often present solutions to disputants as their own—when the solutions were actually generated by one or both of the parties themselves!

A lot of conflicts emerge before the ideas are even presented, because we don't like the messenger. If the other party is suggesting this, then by definition it can't be good for me. One of the first demonstrations of this effect was done during the Cold War era, by examining how Americans reacted to ideas allegedly authored by their own country's diplomats and advisors versus the (then) USSR. In one study, 320 Americans were presented with fifty different proposals about how to end the Cold War that were allegedly put forth by either U.S. or Soviet diplomats.[18] In actual fact, authorship had been assigned randomly to each proposal. Nevertheless, there was a strong devalue-the-author effect: On nearly every proposal— forty-six out of fifty—attitudes were driven by the alleged author of the proposal, not the proposal's content itself! Moreover, differences in support ranged as high as 4 points on a 6-point "likeability" scale, suggesting a strong effect!

The devalue-the-author (a.k.a. kill the messenger) effect is so strong that it applies to colleagues in the same organization as well: "Well, if the sales team likes it, then it can't be good for engineering"; "If the corporate team is on board, then it's not good for R&D."

The hack is, once again, to generate ideas for conflict resolution that remove the author. This is in fact what skilled mediators do to resolve conflict. They interview the disputants separately, collect ideas for conflict resolution, and then present those ideas to the other party while making the ideas appear as the mediators' own.

Given that most of us do not have the funds (or time) to employ third-party mediators, we need a hack. I used a variation of this technique during a particularly bitter and contentious internal company negotiation. Six company divisions battled on several issues. Whenever someone would pitch a proposal or solution, it would quickly be shot down by the other groups.

"Look," I said as the conflict reached a fever pitch, "I'm going to ask everyone to privately write down some solutions—at least four. My rule is that you put one idea on each index card and you cannot sign your name. I don't want to know whose ideas these are. I just want to see the ideas." In essence, I gave the standard brainwriting instructions. For the next ten minutes, the only sound in the room was pens scratching on the index cards I had supplied. I collected over twenty-five cards from the parties involved. To prevent any handwriting analysis, I sent everyone on a twenty-minute break and quickly typed up the ideas from the cards in random order on an Excel sheet, labeling them A, B, C, etc. When the groups returned, I presented the Excel sheet, gave each person four Post-it notes, and told them to vote for their top four ideas that were not their own. Frankly, I had no way of enforcing the don't-vote-for-yourself rule, but they seemed to abide by this because within fifteen minutes, seven ideas had more than three votes each.

We then continued to elaborate on each of the top seven ideas, recombining them and then doing more "secret" voting on the new versions. By the end of this process we had a solution that everyone felt very good about.

HACK 19 >>>>>>>>>>>>>>>>>>>>>>>>>>>>>>>>>>>>>>

Hot-Warm-Cold

I've witnessed a lot of internal negotiations break down over a single word: "No." No is a showstopper for several reasons. First, it is a negative word that people react to strongly. Second, and more importantly, it doesn't allow the receiver to learn anything.

In my negotiation research, I've coached people to use the "hot-warm-cold" method instead of the "yes-no" tactic. Here is how hot-warm-cold works: One party makes several proposals (that are of equal value to them) and asks the other party to rank them in terms of attractiveness; the protagonists agree to set aside questions of "acceptability" and instead focus on rank order.

A gastroenterologist physician, let's call him Doc Gastro, used the hot-warm-cold method to strategize about growing his private practice. Doc Gastro enjoyed about 60 percent of the colonoscopy business in his local market; the next largest practice was run by a good friend—Doc Friend—who had about 16 percent of the colonoscopy market; a large hospital system had the market's remainder. When Doc Gastro approached Doc Friend about a partnership, Doc Friend was intrigued because combining forces would give them over 75 percent of the regional colonoscopy market. Doc Gastro wanted to move this negotiation away from a haggle session, where "no" might be a showstopper or, even worse, motivate Doc Friend to join forces with the local hospital competitor.

So, Doc Gastro prepared for the meeting with Doc Friend by presenting three proposals that he called options A, B, and C.

Doc Gastro constructed each option to be of equal value (all things considered) to Doc Gastro himself. This was the critical part. The idea was to encourage Doc Friend to consider the three proposals and choose the best for him, resulting in a win-win! The proposals involved: (A) Doc Friend selling equity in his practice and becoming a salaried employee; (B) flipping Doc Friend's equity into Doc Gastro's practice without Doc Friend becoming a salaried employee; or (C) selling Doc Friend's practice to Doc Gastro. Ultimately, Doc Friend liked option A. To this day, the two doctors enjoy over 75 percent of the market share with their combined practice!

HACK 20 >>

Interim Deal

In many business situations, the complexity of the deal can bog down negotiations and motivate parties to involve attorneys. And when attorneys show up, the time required to reach agreements can often be daunting and expensive! At the same time, not reaching a deal can be a lose-lose enterprise if parties are not moving forward in a meaningful way.

In such situations, the "interim deal" hack can save the day. Here's how it works: Parties agree to a temporary solution on a subset of the issues, with the clear understanding that the terms are only valid through a mutually agreed-upon date.

After that period, the parties have the option to continue, expand, or terminate the interim deal. Gillespie and Bazerman call such deals a "pre-settlement settlement."[19]

When I mentioned this technique to Tom, a doctor and former executive student of mine, it opened up a possibility for him. Tom has a private practice in a small college town, and enjoys a large market share of a routine medical procedure. The large university hospital does a very small percentage of this routine treatment, and they were interested in buying new equipment because theirs is slow and inefficient. When the chief operating officer of the hospital approached Tom about buying a minority interest in his practice while delaying buying the needed equipment, Tom was not inclined to sell, but agreed to listen to their offer. Moreover, realizing that the process would require months of discovery, signing NDAs, and the like, Tom proposed that in the interim the hospital send their patients to Tom's practice and both parties share the revenues. Tom realized that this would allow the hospital to delay making a major capital purchase for equipment while enabling both the hospital and himself to make more revenue in the interim period. The hospital agreed to the proposal.

HACK 21 >>>>>>>>>>>>>>>>>>>>>>>>>>>>>>>>>>>>>

Zoom Out

Social scientists have found that people tend to be about two to three feet away from each other while conversing. This proximity can often set the stage for a contentious interaction, especially if parties are angry or feel threatened. Indeed, negotiators who face obstacles head-on tend to get stuck and are less able to create win-win solutions.[20] So what's the hack? The key in this case is to use the zoom out strategy, to gain the thirty-thousand-foot view versus the three-foot view. Now, let's be practical. Most of us can't literally ascend to a higher position when we find ourselves in a stressful face-to-face encounter. So, the zooming out here is supposed to be mental. For example, in one investigation, people in a conflict situation were prompted to take either a "distal" (e.g., ten years from now) or "proximal" (e.g., next month) time perspective. Everyone was in the same conflict situation, but those prompted to take the distal view reached more sweet spot agreements. I know of one executive who actually looks up at the sky—literal blue-sky thinking—whenever he feels stuck, to gain a broader, more helpful perspective!

A different senior manager told me how she used the zoom out hack to resolve a conflict in her professional services client team. The conflict was about role assignments for account team members dealing with a high-profile client. One teammate in particular didn't like his assignment, believing it represented low-level, administrative work that didn't use his full skillset. When the group leader sat down with the disgruntled team member, she pointed out that over the next twelve months several new accounts with high-profile clients would be launched, and that team members (like him!) should prioritize which of these accounts might best benefit from their skills. By zooming out to look at the entire portfolio of clients, the leader successfully changed the mindset of the disgruntled team member from frustrated to optimistic.

The zoom out hack is based upon construal theory, which argues that when facing problems or challenges, people either adopt a telephoto (zoom in) or wide-angle mental lens (zoom out).[21] These are known as low- and high-level construal, respectively. As you've probably surmised, it's usually advisable to take a zoom out (wide-angle lens, high-level construal) view. Why? When we use a zoom in view, we don't see the whole picture!

The zoom out hack also works in non-face-to-face situations. For example, in one research investigation people reached more sweet spot deals when they negotiated with someone who they believed was physically far away (several thousand feet away) rather than nearby (just a few feet away).[22] Why? When we believe we are far away from someone or something, we are more likely to take a more holistic view of the situation, and not to get entangled in the details. Indeed, people are more likely to focus on secondary features (issues) than primary features (interests) when their psychological distance is low rather than high.[23] By increasing psychological distance, people are more likely to see the sweet spot in the forest and avoid getting stuck behind a tree.

Researchers Elizabeth Mannix and colleagues suspected that people in long-term relationships could create more sweet spots when they took a wide-angle or long-term view.[24] To examine this, Mannix studied both agreements within a *static* negotiating period and those achieved *dynamically*, or across several negotiations. The idea was that when people took a long-term view, they could reach more creative, win-win arrangements. The researchers created a simulation to allow for the possibility of a moderately advantageous integrative (sweet spot) agreement within each static negotiation, as well as a superior integrative (sweet spot) agreement across negotiations.

The key twist in the study was manipulation of whether the managers believed that they would interact with the other person in the future. Indeed, when managers believed that they would see each other again, they reached more win-win agreements across negotiations. However, when there was uncertainty about their long-term relationship, they took a short-term view, were more intransigent, and were more likely to miss the larger sweet spot deal! Specifically, when managers believed that there was only a 1 percent chance they would *not* see each other again, (i.e., a 99 percent chance they would see each other again), they found the sweet spot. However, when they believed that there was a 25 percent chance they would not see each other again (a 75 percent chance they would see each other again), they were not willing to make a short-term sacrifice in hopes of a bigger future gain. Overall, zooming out to the longer-term view helped managers find the sweet spot more easily.

HACK 22 >>>

Pre-shake

In many cultures, including the U.S. and beyond, people shake hands at the close of a business deal. Shaking hands is a type of psychological contract that can be seen as just as good and valid as a signed document.

However, shaking hands goes well beyond the psychological and symbolic—it releases a powerful dose of oxytocin, the bonding hormone! More broadly, when we are face-to-face, four channels of communication are available to us: the verbal, the paraverbal (how something is said), the visual, and the kinetic (touch). Don't underestimate any of these. For example, in one study, some negotiators were asked to shake hands *before* negotiation, while others were not.[25] Everything else was the same. Guess what? The negotiators who shook hands beforehand created better deals and felt better. Why? Oxytocin!

Don't underestimate the importance of oxytocin in a conflict situation. A large-scale study revealed that oxytocin provides three unique benefits that help people reach sweet spot deals.[26] First, the hormone prompts people to regard those around them as in-group versus out-group members (i.e., the feeling of "We are in this together"). Second, oxytocin dampens amygdala activity (related to fear and similar emotional responses) and increases trust. Third, oxytocin up-regulates neural circuitries that are essential for empathy.

In one investigation, for example, males involved in a contentious conflict exercise were administered either oxytocin or a placebo.[27] Men who received oxytocin took actions to protect their team, even when their own outcomes were not threatened, indicating that oxytocin fueled an empathic desire to safeguard vulnerable group members. Now, it is not very practical (or ethical) for any of us to inject our colleagues and competitors with oxytocin to improve our odds of finding the sweet spot. So we need a hack! The best non-chemical hack is human connection, via a handshake or the equivalent.

I witnessed a variation of the pre-shake in a class I taught. One pair of negotiators realized that each had tattoos on their upper arms, and rubbed their tattoos together before the discussion. Needless to say, they reached a great deal compared to those of most other pairs! Once again, the power of oxytocin at work!

In one of my executive classes, I wanted to see whether a simple greeting prior to a negotiation exercise would set the stage for sweet spot deals. I instructed managers to "find another person in the room and greet them as you would a dear friend." At first many were hesitant. But soon enough there was lots of hugging, handshaking, and European-style cheek-to-cheek greetings! As expected, in the exercise that followed, the managers created an impressive number of sweet spot deals!

So think of shaking hands or some other physical bonding activity, both before and after a negotiation, as a powerful part of your toolkit. Because that's exactly what it is.

*　　*　　*

The sweet spot hacks for resolving workplace conflict can be used with colleagues and coworkers in informal, everyday negotiations. These strategies can also be applied in more formal business situations with clients, customers, and companies.

Workplace negotiations often appear adversarial and much conventional wisdom fuels the belief that people need to be tough-as-nails so they don't get taken advantage of. In truth, most business situations contain a sweet spot, but we won't find it unless we surface some of the key information that people are intent upon concealing. In this sense, there is a catch-22: in order to find the sweet spot, we need information, but people don't disclose information because they fear it will be disadvantageous.

The hacks in this chapter provide a solution to the catch-22 by encouraging people to signal their values, interests, and preferences in a way that does not put them at a bargaining disadvantage and will in fact pave the way for mutual gains.

CHAPTER SEVEN

Sweet Spot Hacks for Virtual Life

THE COVID-19 PANDEMIC THAT BEGAN IN EARLY 2020 FORCED schools to close, community life to shutter, and millions to work from home. Overnight, the entire developed world transitioned from in-person to virtual interactions.

Consider Sandie, a mid-level manager and pre-COVID model employee. When she began working from home—a small condo she shared with her spouse (also telecommuting), three young children, and a Labrador—things fell apart. Sandie had to cancel or delegate leading many video team meetings due to family obligations, frustrating her team and herself. Another manager, Asha, who joined her company just a week before "lockdown" orders, was challenged to lead a global, cross-functional team she had never met in person. Asha was strangely exhausted after daily back-to-back video conference calls. That's no surprise! The "constant gaze" of video meetings, combined with the fact that we can't "choose our seats," raises our stress level.[1]

It's been said that face-to-face business teams are like Ferrari cars—high performance but high maintenance. Virtual teams are akin to Lamborghini Venenos—even more costly and even higher maintenance!

The majority of people—58 percent, in fact—prefer text messages to communicate with others; but only 48 percent engage in face-to-face communication.[2] Texting is now the single most-used feature on any smartphone, with each of us sending an average of thirty-two texts a day in the U.S. alone.[3] If you are a Millennial or a Gen Z, you are twenty times more likely never to speak to your residential neighbors than Baby Boomers (age fifty-five and over).[4]

Not surprisingly, email and other virtual communication modes are increasingly used to negotiate deals that were once conducted face-to-face. One partner at a Boston law firm stated: "Associates lay out their suite of technologies: laptops, iPods, and multiple phones. And then they put their earphones on, big ones. Like pilots. They turn their desks into cockpits."[5]

However, texting can be a source of strain and stress. One study found that the more men text with a partner, the *less* happy they tend to be.[6] Or consider how texting others affects a relationship. Sameer and Sarita Sheth, a couple profiled in a 2016 *New York Times* article, both have irritations with the other about their texting habits. Sarita is guilty of checking her phone during family dinners, and Sameer routinely texts others on Saturday mornings, which makes Sarita feel like he is not being present in family time: "Because when he's home, it's our time. I want him to be here." And by that she means mentally, not just physically.[7]

When it comes to advice about communication "e-tiquette," one popular website suggests that couples follow some basic rules, such as: (1) "speak up," which roughly translates into actually sending a response when you read your partner's text. Why? When people see the "read" message but don't get a response, they can become agitated and distracted; (2) "sign-off," which essentially means letting your partner know when you are putting the phone on mute or off to attend a meeting or focus on work; (3) "no fighting" (it's as simple as, "I don't want to fight over text. Let's talk about this when we see each other"); (4) be "meaningful," which means that messages should contain some substance (show your partner you care by saying something thoughtful).[8]

The mere act of checking email creates stress and elevates levels of cortisol, the stress hormone.[9] In one study, 132 people answered questions over an eight-day period: four days when they were expected to be available for work, and four when they weren't. In that survey period, half of the participants had saliva samples measured for cortisol. During the times when a person was expected to be reachable (i.e., when they were in "work mode"), they had elevated cortisol levels and felt stressed. And even when they were not required to be *available* for work but were *accessible* via email and phone, they still showed significant cortisol increases. Not surprisingly, some companies have instituted "email boundaries," or norms that prohibit employees from sending work-related emails outside of regular work hours. They work: a ten-year study on the effectiveness of email boundaries shows that they improve employee engagement.[10] Yet email boundaries are hard to enforce. Just the mere expectation that one might get an off-hours communication triggers anxiety.[11] Checking work email after hours is severely damaging to people's mental health, and "flexible work hours" has spiraled into "work with no boundaries."[12]

Moreover, most of us have not had formal training in virtual communication for the workplace; we are essentially "winging it." Even if someone is skilled in face-to-face communication, this does not guarantee that they will be effective with the virtual variety. To be sure, most people prefer to negotiate face-to-face, but what may work well in a face-to-face situation may not be effective in a virtual situation, or could even be detrimental and backfire. Consider what happened to Talia Jane, a twenty-five-year-old customer support representative with Eat24, the Yelp food delivery app.[13] Frustrated with her low pay, she wrote an open letter to her CEO—in the form of a two-thousand-word blog. Within two hours, her work email was disabled and she received a phone call from human resources with bad news: "We feel it's best to part ways." In this situation, Talia's virtual open letter backfired. Other cases of young managers fired on the spot because they sent their grievances via email have occurred. When it comes to complaints and grievances, face-to-face or over the phone remain the preferred options.

To find the sweet spot in our virtual interaction means using new tools. Salespeople trained in traditional face-to-face techniques must use different strategies when interacting online/virtually. For example, one sales training program solemnly cautions, "old school selling is on the brink of extinction."[14] The message is that what got you where you are today won't necessarily ensure your future success, especially in the virtual world.

Because virtual communication is a critical part of our lives, it is worthwhile to understand how our own behaviors may unwittingly set the stage for a negative or positive outcome when seated at the virtual negotiation table.

So, where do people trip up when negotiating virtually? A big key is trust. When we communicate face-to-face, we build trust nonconsciously, facilitated by a symphony of nonverbal behaviors. We are not aware of all the micro-adjustments we are making in the moment, and how these small but important adaptations lay (or fail to lay) the foundation of trust.[15]

When we communicate face-to-face, we have several channels of communication available to us: visual, verbal, paraverbal, and kinetic. Visual means we can see the other party's facial expressions and body language. We know that raised eyebrows signals surprise or disbelief, and crossed arms reveal a desire to create distance. We listen not only to what our communication partner is saying (verbal), but also *how* they are communicating (paraverbal). For example, we can detect sarcasm and mockery fairly easily.

"Kinetic" refers to physical touch—we touch each other much more than we realize when communicating. A light touch on the arm, a handshake, and so on can affect the course of conflict resolution significantly.

In sum, our brains process a lot of visual, auditory, and kinetic information, allowing us to adapt, shape, and revise our communication in real time, much like driving a car: In communication, we figuratively speed up, slow down, take a different route, and so on as a function of hazards and other immediate stimuli. Meanwhile, our conversational partner is likely doing the same thing. Facial expressions, nonverbal behaviors, body posture, touching, and social distance coordinate in systematic ways to enhance the process of communication.[16] This is known as the *dance of communication*. Skilled communicators are particularly good at making the other person feel comfortable and in sync.

Trust is the glue for many negotiations, and trust is built differently when we communicate online. When we are face-to-face, trust is built on more psychological factors, like similarity and nonverbal gestures. However, when we communicate virtually, trust—at least initially—is driven more by perceived competence and expertise.[17]

To be sure, technology-mediated communication has a number of benefits that most likely outweigh the costs. The key is to know what can go wrong ahead of time and set the stage for sweet spot interactions to occur. That means it's time for some e-customized hacks!

The Big Five
E-communication Whammies

We need specific hacks to lay the foundation for finding the sweet spot in our e-communications. I created the relevant hacks to navigate what I refer to as the "big five e-communication whammies." These big whammies often blindside us because we have not anticipated how our good-faith attempts to communicate via email, text, chat, or even conference call might be distorted or perceived in an unintended way by our communication recipients. By understanding how our own behavior changes when we are not face-to-face, we can make adjustments so that our communication is perceived as intended.

Whammy #1: Doctor Jekyll and Mr. Hyde

One Silicon Valley company wanted to minimize their superfluous meetings and conversations, and decided to hold all meetings via email, citing efficiency as the goal.[18] Over the course of a few weeks, tension among employees in the company skyrocketed, and people problems that had not previously existed cropped up everywhere. What this company failed to realize is that face-to-face conversation acts as a social lubricant. Casual conversations, such as about the weather and sports, that don't seem to pertain directly to strategy, goal-setting, or performance progress lay the foundation for more substantive conversations. Think of casual face-to-face conversation as the load-bearing walls that hold up the structure of many relationships.

In general, many companies and CEOs started to realize recently that as much as email facilitates communication across time and distance, it can also create "cyber-monsters." That is, people *behave differently* when they are using email or text; they are more likely to insult others, use aggressive language, and make threats. Moreover, people on the receiving end are more likely to take offense when the communication is virtual. I call this the "Dr. Jekyll and Mr. Hyde" effect, meaning that the same person might seem to undergo a complete personality change when communicating face-to-face versus email. Practically speaking, this means that a small concern raised in a face-to-face conversation might appear to be a huge problem when communicated via email. Similarly, a clarifying question in a face-to-face encounter might appear harmless, but the same question by email may come across as a direct attack. What explains why people become more Hyde-like when they communicate via email?

Social disinhibition is a psychological term that refers to the fact that people are *less* inhibited when communicating virtually as opposed to face-to-face. So a person might be willing to say something virtually that they would hesitate to say in person. Usually this verbalizing is a criticism or something negative. On the one hand, people are encouraged to "speak their mind," but when our inhibitions are lowered, we are likely to say things that might be perceived as harsh or downright cruel. This social disinhibition in virtual contexts used to be called "flaming"—when someone writes a caustic remark or rebuttal to someone—and is often anonymous.[19] Flaming often leads to more flaming, and each party sees themselves as an innocent victim reacting to the other party's inappropriate behavior in a fast-escalating spiral.

Consider what happened to Patrick Evershed, who sent a formal complaint letter via email to his company's human resources department regarding his boss, London financier John Duffield, requesting that Duffield be removed.[20] After employers received the letter, Evershed was promptly summoned by Duffield, who gave him fifteen minutes to clear his desk and also warned, "this might be very expensive for you."

Some leaders we know have developed personal policies for when and how to send emails. One leader never sends an email after 9:00 p.m. unless it's "very dull." He also sends the email to himself and saves it as a draft. Informed by past regretful experiences, he developed six rules of thumb for emailing:[21]

1. Turn the email box off (don't immediately read and respond to emails).
2. Never criticize anyone in an email, and avoid technical debates.
3. Be judicious about who the email is sent to and who is copied.
4. Observing some formality is important.
5. Review and revise important emails.
6. Remember that email is a public and permanent record.

Another problem with virtual communication is the unintended recipient. It is highly doubtful that anyone would walk up to the wrong person in the office and communicate about a sensitive topic; but think about how often you've accidently sent an email to the wrong person via an innocent auto-fill-in keystroke or the dreaded accidental "reply all." Alice, an employee at a business, received an email from her boss that was actually intended for one of his same-level colleagues. The email was complaining about Alice's late arrival time in the office.[22] In this case, Alice wasn't sure how to respond; she struggled with whether to bring it up with the boss. Should she ignore it? Well, that was hard because she felt that she wanted to clear the air about the company's promise of flexible hours. Also, it was probably just a matter of time until the boss realized that the intended recipient was not responding. This is a problem specific to the virtual domain.

In general, why are people less inhibited when communicating virtually versus face-to-face? The reason is that our brains function quite differently when we are not in the presence of others. Most people experience a release of oxytocin (the bonding hormone) when around others. That's not the case when we're communicating via phone or computer.

Moreover, mutual gaze—where we look into another person's eyes—triggers certain centers of the brain to make us behave in a more compassionate fashion. This all changes when we communicate virtually, so our brain is literally not getting the same signals and we behave in a more self-interested fashion.

Whammy #2: Gray-colored Glasses Effect

Social disinhibition is bad enough, but the "gray-colored glasses effect" is like pouring gasoline on the fire. This effect is the tendency for people communicating virtually to perceive everything more negatively. Both senders and receivers see the negative. This means that a positive message is seen as neutral; a neutral message is seen as negative; and a negative message is viewed as, well, downright incendiary!

In general, the blunt, sometimes harsh communication that occurs when people are not face-to-face results from what's known as the "negativity effect."[23] This means that when we find ourselves embroiled in a conflict situation, communicating virtually may amplify negative emotion and escalate the situation. Why? In the absence of the behavioral cues we use to adjust our communication, we may switch into automatic pilot or overdrive to attempt to address conflict. So it's not surprising that people have a harder time reaching amicable agreements when they are not face-to-face. What they don't necessarily realize is that their very behavior changes—they transform from a Dr. Jekyll into a Mr. Hyde, as discussed earlier. Lacking self-awareness, they blame the other party when things start to go south.

This difference between face-to-face and other forms of communication was seen most starkly in a study of human resource managers giving performance reviews.[24] In all cases, the person being evaluated was identical—they had the same performance record. The question was: When it came to offering this person feedback on their job performance, would there be marked differences when the feedback was delivered face-to-face (i.e., synchronously) or via written note (i.e., asynchronously)? Reviewers provided much harsher feedback when communicating via written note rather than face-to-face. Presumably, they simply were communicating their honest opinions, without fear of direct reprisal. However, when communicating face-to-face, they hedged and cloaked their messages.

We are also more likely to experience rejection when asking for something by email versus asking for the same thing in person. This is because when people make a request via email, they overestimate their persuasiveness and then are disappointed if the recipient says no.[25] Part of our inability to "read" the situation is that we don't take the perspective of the party on the receiving end of our request.

In general, then, the point is to remember most of us wear gray-colored glassed when engaging in virtual or other non-face-to-face communication, and to try to adjust the communication—or its receipt—accordingly.

Whammy #3: P-charisma versus E-charisma

Recently I sat in on a class taught by a business communication coach. Just before class I asked him to tell me what "charisma" means. He said it simply means "how someone fills up a space." "Can you give me an example?" I asked. Sure, he said, as we walked into the classroom. He pointed out several students who were talking to classmates: a tall, athletic male student with a perfectly tailored suit and a stentorian voice; a young woman with a bright smile and infectious laugh; another woman wearing a pair of dark glasses placed thoughtfully mid-nose and using her arms and hands illustratively as she spoke. All of these people had what the executive coach referred to as classic "charisma"—something that I've come to call "P-charisma," or "physical" charisma—the way they stand, walk, move, dress, gesture, nod, and so on. P-charisma is based largely on just what my colleague said—how people fill up a physical space.

In a typical face-to-face meeting, P-charisma is very important. Why? The scarcest resource in such a business meeting is *time*. Getting time to speak is a precious and rare resource and so there is obvious competition for the floor, where more dominant personalities attempt to overpower others. When one person is speaking, others typically fall silent and gaze at the speaker. When the speaker is ready to relinquish their speaking turn, they look back at the group or a given person. When another speaker wants to interject and take control of the conversation, they make an obvious physical gesture, clear their throat, or adjust their posture. A similar dynamic emerges in the traditional classroom. Competition for speaking time is played out through a complex battle of nonverbal and paraverbal cues. Often, it is the people with physical charisma (P-charisma)—extraverted, physically expressive people who exude confidence—who carry most of the conversation.

What about e-communication? When people communicate via information technology, competition for the floor does not exist. Because communication is often asynchronous, people do not have to compete for airtime. They can write, post, and deliver messages on their own terms. It is not physical charisma, characterized by body language and good looks, that determines influence, then, but a different type of charisma, something I call "E-charisma": electronic charisma, which is how a person uses technology-based messaging. E-charisma involves a completely different set of skills and attributes than does P-charisma. And for people who've enjoyed the benefits of P-charisma most of their lives, E-charisma might not come naturally. Thus, a different pecking order arises in the virtual world.

I noticed this phenomenon firsthand in my own MBA teaching. To be sure, most of our courses are delivered in a traditional classroom that seats thirty to seventy-five students. I find that in that context the most verbally dominant students are usually those who are extraverts, well-networked within their cohorts, and high in social confidence—often men. Having said that, these people might not actually have the best ideas or insights. When I started to teach online courses, in which students don't have to compete for the floor via P-charisma, I observed an interesting phenomenon. The students who generated the most attention on the class discussion board were typically not those high in P-charisma—i.e., they were not the highly verbal, physically dominant, charismatic communicators. In fact, some were downright shy in the presence of others. Rather, it was the power of their ideas that determined their influence in the class—their E-charisma. By the standards of the communication coach, these people do not have "charisma," at least in a stage-presence kind of way; instead they have E-charisma, which means that they possess a thoughtful, punchy communication style and a flair for expression that makes the reader think, "Wow, they said so well exactly what I was thinking."

Whammy #4: Get Down to Business

One thing I've observed about meetings that aren't face-to-face is that people don't waste any time getting down to business. For example, on one occasion I asked a client if I could (silently) observe his onsite, in-person meeting to get a sense of the communication dynamics in play. I observed a lot of joking, laughter, and easy conversation during the minutes before the meeting started. People were talking about their weekends and pulling up and sharing pictures on their phones. When the meeting started, people got more serious, but there were also some dips into laughter. I also noticed an interesting interchange of nonverbal communication—winks, nods, mutual glances, inside jokes, and the like.

I desperately wanted a comparison group, so I asked my contact if I could listen in on a conference call meeting with his geographically dispersed regional team the next week. I willingly signed an NDA, and my host introduced me during the call (so people knew I was there); then the conference call meeting proceeded. Unlike the face-to-face meeting I had observed earlier, there was an immediate focus on the task, with minimal laughter or joking. There were several instances in which two or more people attempted to speak at the same time, followed by longer-than-normal silences. We also heard several background noises—one caller seemed to be having a separate meeting in their home office while simultaneously attending the conference call!

The idea, then, is that meetings that aren't face-to-face tend to be more serious and offer more opportunity for miscues and distraction, so resist the urge to immediately get down to business, and instead add in the human factor. Case in point: One remote worker takes pictures of himself every day and emails it to his virtual team saying, "thought you would want to see what shirt I was wearing today."[26]

Whammy #5: Ghosting

"Ghosting" is a term that refers to, well, literally ignoring someone. Ghosting is the practice of ending a personal relationship with someone by suddenly and without explanation withdrawing from all communication. Ghosting is not easy to do in person, but it is much easier when communicating virtually. It may seem strange to think that people would ghost a colleague or client that they presumably have a relationship with. But this happens all the time.

Consider three types of ghosting that my students and clients have shared with me: (1) "outright ghosting," when someone completely ignores your email message or text communication; (2) "slow ghosting," where a conspicuously lengthy amount of time occurs before they respond to your email, text, or phone call; and (3) "change-the-subject ghosting," where the recipient selectively responds only to certain parts of your message or query, and never addresses the most critical issue or question. Not surprisingly, all three types of ghosting elevate suspicion and stress.

Note that any of these three types of ghosting would be nearly impossible to do in a traditional face-to-face interaction; so people need to develop methods to deal with e-ghosting. I refer to these intervention techniques as "ghostbusters"! The most common ghostbuster technique involves resending your email with a subject line like "Second request" or "Friendly reminder," thereby attempting to provoke the recipient to respond. Another type of ghostbuster tactic is a face-to-face reminder of the e-communication. "I sent you an email," a colleague said to me in the elevator one morning—the subtext, of course, was, "I know you got my message; why haven't you responded?" To be sure, once "busted," I ran back to my office and replied to the email.

Okay. Now that we are aware of the "big five whammies," let's outline some hacks that can ward off some of the negative outcomes that could emerge. Warning: Reading this chapter will probably make you extremely self-conscious about your online communication style!

Schmooze or Lose
(or the Virtual Handshake)

"Schmooze or Lose." That was the title of the first article I published with my colleagues in the area of e-negotiation. [27] My fascination with this subject started when a client confided that his most important negotiations with customers did not take place face-to-face, but rather via email, text, and sometimes phone calls. My client pleaded with me to give him some best practices to add to his toolkit.

This conversation prompted me to contact my colleague, Professor Michael Morris (at Stanford Business School at the time) who was preparing to teach a negotiation course during the same term I was scheduled to teach Kellogg MBA students. With the growing ubiquity of virtual and distance negotiation and teamwork challenges (like that faced by my client), Michael Morris, Janice Nadler, Terri Kurtzberg, and I collaborated to examine whether business negotiations conducted via email might diminish people's ability to find and create sweet spot deals. So, we set up a high-stakes business negotiation situation in which everyone was paired with a counterparty to negotiate via email.

In the simulation, our students (from Stanford and Kellogg) negotiated against each other via email in a realistic business situation: The parties were told they were all members of the same company, but they were geographically dispersed—just as some large, international companies have managers located in different offices and different functions. We paired up the students randomly in a one-on-one negotiation. To make the situation even more realistic, their performance in the negotiation mattered: Each role-playing business leader had their own profit center and was incentivized to maximize the value they created.

Because the negotiation simulation was complex and high-stakes, we gave each student manager a full week to conduct the negotiation (via email) with their counterpart. They had complete liberty to email the counterparty as they wished during that seven-day period. Shortly before the email negotiation was to begin, we added a twist: Some people were instructed to have a short (i.e., less than five minutes) phone call prior to commencing their virtual negotiation. Others were not asked to do that. This was the only point of difference between the two groups. Moreover, we cautioned that the phone call was to be strictly social; they were not to discuss the business matter at hand, but any kind of small talk was permitted. For the next week, all the young managers attempted to resolve the thorny, high-stakes business conflict. After the weeklong exchange, they sent us their full email-exchange transcripts for analysis.

The result? Negotiators who did not have the five-minute phone call were much less likely to reach sweet spot deals; in fact, the majority of them failed to reach a deal at all! They declared a deadlock or impasse at a much higher rate (61 percent) than did those who had the brief up-front call (40 percent). Even though the phone call had nothing to do with the business at hand, it created a foundation of rapport and trust for the negotiators. Five minutes of small talk, in this case, successfully warded off lose-lose outcomes.

Moreover, the analysis of the email transcripts revealed that some of the negotiations had gone south almost immediately. In many cases it was the ghosting issue mentioned earlier: "I sent you an email six hours ago, and you have not responded." In others, the email messages started to take on a terse, almost telegraphic quality: "Respond now or else we will not move forward." Understandably, such messages were viewed as thinly veiled threats.

Intrigued, I showed the findings to an economist friend. (Let me preface what comes next by saying that many of my good friends are economists.) My friend looked at the results and said, "These people are not behaving rationally." I asked him to explain. The economist pointed out that the five-minute conversation was "cheap talk," meaning that it had no binding impact and therefore should not affect the negotiation results. To be sure, several economists I know use that exact expression to emphasize that in the absence of binding contracts, people can say anything they want and make promises that should be largely dismissed because there is no underlying enforceable obligation.[28] Now, it seemed to me that in our investigation the cheap talk was not cheap at all, meaning that the managers in the study who had the phone call ended up with more sweet spot deals and created significantly greater financial value for their organizations! So, we needed to dig even deeper to understand the impact of seemingly meaningless, nonbinding conversation on negotiation performance.

Unlike our economist friends, my colleagues and I believed that "cheap talk" acts as a social glue or lubrication that might pave the way for sweet spot deals. Sure, cheap talk is not technically binding in a *legal* sense, as the economists point out, but people often *act as though* it is. Many people use the term "handshake deal" to refer to the fact that they have verbally agreed to terms but there is no associated legal binding commitment. In such instances, talk is hardly cheap.

To test this "talk-is-not-cheap" idea, my colleagues and I teamed with an economist on a study to examine how competitive and cooperative people behave in a negotiation situation in which it is *tempting for people to lie or conceal information*.[29] We devised three sets of rules to determine how they might affect the negotiation's process and outcome. In the "cheap talk" condition, parties were allowed to talk face-to-face prior to making a private decision (i.e., to either be nice or "screw" the other person); in the "written note" condition, participants were only allowed to send a written note; and a final "no communication" group was not allowed any pre-game communication. The economist predicted that there would be no differences in the outcomes for these three groups. Why? Because people in the "cheap talk" and "written note" group could *say* anything they dang well pleased prior to making a choice, but then turn around and do anything they wanted when it came down to making an actual decision, because their earlier words were not binding. To make it even more tempting to engage in truly cheap talk, we devised a method in which people would never actually have to see their opponent, because they would arrive and leave through separate entrances and exits.

As you might guess, my behavioral science colleagues and I had a very different prediction than our economist counterparts. Even though the talk was not binding, and participants would never even encounter the other person in the future, we suspected that those in the richer communication conditions would be more likely to keep their word and reach sweet spot deals than would the no-communication people.

That is indeed what happened, a big surprise to the economists! People who communicated face-to-face or in writing were more than twice as likely to follow through on their promises—even though they had no obligation to do so. Hence the "cheap talk" in this case paved the way toward mutual trust, proving it was far from cheap in reality!

HACK 24 >>

Communication Cholesterol (Watch Your Ratio)

I find it useful to think about your e-communication like cholesterol, meaning that there are two kinds of conversational tones: positive and negative. Positive-toned communication is conveyed in phrases such as "This is great," "I really like . . . ," and "Thank you so much," through greetings ("Dear So-and-So") and closings ("Best wishes"), and also in emojis such as smiley faces and the use of exclamation points.

Negative-toned communication is conveyed through negations and other phrases like "I don't think . . ." and "This is a problem" and the even harsher "I am not happy with . . ."

When it comes down to it, it is the ratio of positive-to-negative that is really important for our e-communication, not the absolute number of each *per se*. For this reason, I often have businesspeople show me an email chain with a colleague, client, or customer and then underline the negative-toned communication (e.g., "I'm concerned . . . ," "This is not what I was expecting . . . ," "There's a problem . . .") and circle all the positive-toned phrases (e.g., "This is nice . . . ," "I appreciate . . . ," "This is great . . ."). Then I have them count up the circles and the underlines and look at their ratios. This is all part of what's called "emotional engagement."

According to researchers, three types of engagement can be measured via your words: emotional engagement, social engagement, and task engagement.[30] Let's face it: Relationship-building is more difficult over email than face-to-face.[31] One key to building a relationship via e-communication is to be engaged. But how?

As a second step in analyzing your own email communication, count all your pronouns—e.g., "I," "me," "you," "us," "our," "we," etc. Personal pronouns reflect attention to *people* rather than to objects or concepts. The more personal pronouns present, the more people are paying attention to people—themselves as well as others. First-person pronouns are interesting. Whereas using a lot of "I, me, mine" words can reflect a neurotic or ruminative self-focus, in natural conversation it often takes the form of hedging (e.g., "I think this might work . . ."). But it also can reflect dominance. According to researchers Lincke and Ulijn, the ideal rank order of personal pronoun use in negotiation is: first: "you," second: "we," third: " I," and fourth: "they."[32] Your total number of pronouns is a reflection of your social engagement.

Finally, circle all the verbs (action words) in your email ("work," "talk," "meet," "align," etc.). These reflect task engagement. Examine at least three exchanges between you and another person, using these three indexes. Are you engaged? Is the other person engaged? On what dimensions: emotional, social, task?

The hack is twofold. First, do not begin messages with anything negative. Why? This creates a general gloomy tone and negativity in the other person such that everything that follows will be interpreted as negative. So begin with the positive. Second, aim for at least a two-to-one ratio in your positive-negative messaging.

HACK 25 >

Nothing but Good News

Some companies have observed the tendency for communication to bend toward the negative when face-to-face communication is removed, and are taking steps to address this issue. For example, Lars Dalgaard, CEO of SuccessFactors, recognized how asynchronous communication (such as email) can start a negative ripple effect. So he instituted two simple rules: (1) no one can blind carbon copy anyone else on an email; and (2) if somebody starts to "complain" about another team member or employee, Lars will bring that person into the email chain himself.[33] Perhaps it was a similar fear about the creation of cyber-monsters that led one CEO I know to institute a new policy within his company: "Nothing but good news and updates via email."

Several businesses have instituted email norms to improve communication and prevent misunderstanding. For example, *Small Business Trends* suggests ten key email-related principles:[34]

1. Keep it short (most people are skimming emails and don't want to read a dissertation).

2. Make the subject line a summary (don't sound like a spammer, but keep it brief).

3. Start and end with "you" (you want to get your recipient's attention, so begin with "You asked me to . . ." or "You mentioned that we should . . .").

4. Only one topic per message (don't send your reader a laundry list; instead break up emails into a single message for each topic).

5. Use appropriate tone (sarcasm is really hard to pull off correctly; imagine that any email sent is going to be cc'd across the organization).

6. Don't copy everyone in sight (this is a message, not a class-action suit).

7. Respect spelling and grammar (I learned this the hard way when one of my clients asked me if I was in a hurry. I said, "No, why?" He explained that the email messages I'd been sending contained hundreds of errors. Since then, I've turned on spell- and grammar-check, and always proofread before sending).

8. Remember, it's not private (your email technically belongs to your company and could get submitted in court; so for sensitive topics, pick up the phone or have an in-person chat).

9. Email is not for arguments (never argue in an email; asynchronous communication quickly becomes litigious).

10. Watch the threads (start a new email after about three to four turns).

HACK 26 >>>>>>>>>>>>>>>>>>>>>>>>>>>>>>>>>

Language Style Matching

We've all heard of mirroring, which refers to how people attempt to use the same body language of the people they are communicating with (a topic discussed in Hack #9). For example, salespeople are trained to mirror the body language of customers and clients. Several research studies reveal that subtle mirroring works. However, when people communicate via email or text or chat-apps, mirroring body language is not an option. The next best alternative is *linguistic* style matching.

A person's linguistic style refers to how they put their words together. Language style matching (LSM) literally means that people use the same words or phrases another person does, conveying that they hold the same perception of the situation.[35] Using LSM, researchers can measure the degree of similarity in people's language styles, which predicts (among other things), how much they will like each other, build trust, and cooperate.[36] Thus LSM is a simple, unobtrusive means of measuring the stylistic language similarity of people in a conversation. When people's linguistic styles match, they feel a great deal of harmony. People who match each other's language styles in conversation tend to have more positive interactions.[37] One of the most powerful examples of the power of LSM was a study of interactions between President Nixon and his aides.[38] Specifically, examining eighteen linguistic dimensions of language revealed that in the final conversations between Nixon and John Dean (when tensions and suspicion were sky-high) there was little coordination of language and frequent dominance contests, suggesting low LSM.

In another investigation, researchers studied the linguistic styles of diplomats using original data from the plenary sessions of the Constitutional Convention on the Future of the European Union from 2002–2003.[39] When diplomats converged on a shared linguistic style (had a higher LSM), their discussions were more likely to end in agreement; but when their linguistic styles did not converge, their discussions were more likely to result in disagreement.

Language style matching has also been studied in romantic couples, showing that there can be too much of a good thing! In one investigation, couples engaged in a video-recorded discussion. They discussed either a *relationship* stressor or one partner's *personal* stressor (a social support discussion). The more that couples converged on their language, the more the stressed partner felt supported; however, greater levels of LSM led to lower positive emotions for the couples discussing relationship stressors. That is, the more the couples engaged in LSM, the more likely it was that they used critical and negative behaviors.[40] Why? When the couples were discussing relationship stressors, higher LSM amplified the overall negative tone of the interaction. The conclusion: LSM does not uniformly lay the groundwork for rapport, but instead amplifies both the positive and negative tone of interaction. Hack: use language style matching to converge on positive language elements, not negative ones!

Another study examined negotiations conducted via instant message.[41] The negotiating pairs that were higher in LSM were indeed more socially engaged, but were less focused on the task at hand, and were less able to reach a mutually beneficial outcome during the short discussion time. Those people who matched their partner's style early in the interaction (versus later) had more positive interactions.

Language style matching is not as simple as just using the same words as your communication partner. Why? As suggested above, too many negative words can pull partners into a swirl of negativity. One investigation studied the linguistic style of twenty divorce mediation cases.[42] For the successful divorce mediations, those in which the couples reached mutual settlement (a type of sweet spot), the partners had linguistic synchrony for positive empowerment markers. What exactly is an "empowerment marker"? It is quite simply the process of evolving from a weak position—one that signals lack of ability and action to participate in bringing about resolution—to a position of strength by someone who is calm, centered, confident, decisive, and organized. In this sense, a person moves from retreating from conflict to actively and constructively engaging with key issues.

Consider how one couple explained how they moved from weakness to empowerment when they realized that they had been arguing about the same thing for years—namely, how to parent effectively. One of them believed in a "laissez faire" approach; the other was much more strict. During one of their conflicts, their eldest child complained, "Why do you both argue about the same exact thing every week? Neither of you ever changes your mind." One member of the couple proposed that they set aside a time each week to talk about the most important "parenting" issues facing them that week and agree to not bring up past or future situations, a much more empowered approach.

As people become actively engaged with one another, their use of words and phrases signals their perception of the situation, along with their heartfelt concerns and goals. Certain words and phrases are particularly important for creating trust and rapport. A person's language style is defined by their use of function words (e.g., pronouns and articles)—the key words that make up most of the English language.[43] Personal pronouns include, "I," "she," "they," etc., and articles are words such as "a," "an," "the," etc. Function words reflect how a person feels. Unlike content words (such as nouns and verbs), function words have little meaning out of specific context and are processed rapidly and usually unconsciously.[44]

Quite frankly, given all of these features of spoken language, it is difficult to match a person's conversational style at will.[45] So, we need a hack.

One investigation studied whether within-conversation language convergence (i.e., using the same pronouns and articles as one's communication partner) would lead people to like and trust each other in an eight-minute online chat.[46] The results? Within four minutes of interaction, the conversational partners developed a strong preference for whom they wanted to converse with and contact in the future—and their choices were driven by language matching. The most important aspect is *early* matching in the conversation. The hack, then, is to try to become more similar to your conversational partner early in the conversation. In other words, even more important than baseline similarity (how alike two people are when it comes to using language), the critical factor that predicts a successful, positive interaction is convergence—how they *grow together* during the interaction.

A separate investigation explored LSM in high-stakes hostage negotiation situations.[47] Obviously the emotional stakes are high and every minute counts in such situations. As expected, the greater the LSM was, the more successful the negotiations were. In fact, the unsuccessful hostage negotiations often had dramatic fluctuations, with the lead negotiator unable to maintain steady levels of rapport due to low LSM. Each immediate communication and its form mattered. For example, if the police negotiator interacted in short, positive bursts, then the hostage-taker tended to follow suit.

There's even a theory that helps explain the effects of LSM. According to *Communication Accommodation Theory*, people continually alter their behavior to create, maintain, and in some cases, decrease the social distance between themselves and others.[48] Of all the strategies for decreasing social distance (and building a relationship), *convergence* is the one that is the most effective. Convergence occurs when people use the mannerisms, words, and behaviors of the other party—i.e., LSM. Indeed, as people are more in sync (on the same figurative page with one another), they start to match the language style of the other, which in turn brings them closer, as part of a cycle promoting greater harmony.

HACK 27 >>>>>>>>>>>>>>>>>>>>>>>>>>>>>>>>>>>>

A Picture Is Worth a Thousand Words

Some time ago, I was doing my first podcast. The potential audience was huge—"possibly as large as ten thousand people" my host said. Moreover, the podcast time frame seemed long—over an hour—and I was to be speaking about teamwork and negotiation. After I presented a thirty-minute introduction, the host was to pitch me questions. I would not know the questions in advance, and was to respond on the spot. Knowing the research on disinhibition and the negativity effect (we tend to act more negatively when communication is not in person, like a podcast, where the audience can't be seen or heard), I was concerned that I would start to feel disconnected from my audience—or, even worse, I might unwittingly say something too harsh or judgmental.

So, an hour before the podcast was to start, I found a color photograph of a large lecture hall that showed clearly the faces of engaged, friendly students. I printed a large version of the picture and taped it on my wall, right above my computer.

When it came time for the podcast, I made a point of gazing at the students' faces in the photograph—many of them were smiling—and I found myself smiling back and even nodding at them occasionally. I'm sure that any colleagues looking in through my windowed office door thought I was either insane or on hallucinogenic drugs! But my hack worked for me. I had warded off the disinhibition and negativity effect in one fell swoop by placing the photo of the lecture hall on my wall. I had created a human factor to engage key parts of my brain during this important first podcast.

This "photo of real people" hack led to a real, scientific experiment my colleagues and I conducted in which we had student managers do a negotiation via email. Here was the twist: we provided some participants with a thumbnail photo of their opponent.[49] Others were not given a photo. Otherwise, everything about the negotiation was identical between groups. The results clearly showed how important the visual factor—in this case, a very small picture—is for humanizing the interaction. The student managers who received a thumbnail photo of their opponent created more sweet spot deals in their e-negotiations than those who did not receive the photo. Specifically, 96 percent of the negotiators who received the small photo reached a mutual agreement, compared to only 78 percent of the no-photo group. Even more notably, the groups who had a photo created sweet spot deals that totaled $1.68 million more in collective value than the no-photo group!

HACK 28 >>>>>>>>>>>>>>>>>>>>>>>>>>>>>>>>>>>>>

Mirror on the Wall

Sometimes people do not know when their internal Mr. Hyde has taken over their personality. They rampage through their inbox and text chains, caustically dashing off missives, leaving a trail of damaged relationships in their wake. They might do the same on conference calls, too, bullying others without a hint of self-awareness.

Adita, an executive in my class, was extremely distraught about a recent performance review. She leads a virtual team, and her 360-degree feedback was uniformly negative: "She has a brusque, combative style," "does not make others feel valued," and, perhaps most disconcerting, "does not listen to others and forces her own opinion on the group." The most startling thing to my executive student was that she was completely unaware that this was the impression she was making on her virtual team. When Adita approached me for advice, I shifted into my tough-love mode: "Look, this is a 360-degree report, and there is no logical way that all nine people are wrong and you are right."

Adita admitted that she needed to change. I was pleased to hear that, but added that she could not start her personal change journey until she gained some personal awareness. "How am I supposed to do that?" she asked. I told her about a research study that had involved placing mirrors around yourself to gain insight into how your expressions and tone may be seen by others. In this study, people who communicated in front of a mirror were more self-critical and were more ethical in their communication than those who did not use a mirror.[50]

Well, Adita was extremely enterprising and took the idea one step further. She held a meeting with her team and made clear that she had heard the difficult feedback about her leadership style and wanted to make real behavioral changes. She challenged each member of the team to act as her "mirrors" by modeling her body language. What she learned was invaluable—several of her direct reports crossed their arms and shook their heads to convey how she often appeared, helping Adita to adapt more positive communication practices over time. Adita realized that she used the same brusque style in her email communications. With her new awareness of how others perceived her, she became more thoughtful when composing messages.

HACK 29 >>>>>>>>>>>>>>>>>>>>>>>>>>>>>>>>>>>>>

Q&A

Asking questions is a critical success factor in negotiation. My research has shown, for example, that people who ask questions create more sweet spot deals.[51]

One district manager (DM) in a large supplier company conducts a lot of non-face-to-face business negotiations with vendors, customers, and manufacturers. The DM has seen firsthand that when either party begins to make arguments and assertions, it can quickly spiral into a contest of wills. So, the DM developed what he called a "habit" of starting every e-conversation by first asking a question that reiterates the current issues that the customer is dealing with and for which they want a solution. For example, when it comes to deliveries, the DM summarizes what issue the customer brought up in the previous conversation *in the form of a question:* "It sounds like you are very concerned that subcontractors are not onsite in time for deliveries?" and "Am I right that when you don't know if the delivery was made, this is a problem?" The DM has learned that summarizing the customer's concerns from a previous conversation in the form of a question makes the customer feel appreciated and gives them an opportunity to correct any misperceptions.

As a more developed example, here's one summarizing question the DM asked an important customer: "So you mentioned that you have difficulty coordinating deliveries between your subcontractor and your current supplier because one of the parties is late or does not show up, correct?" After asking a question like that to confirm concerns, the DM moves to posing a question about how the customer feels about the current situation: "Those situations ultimately end up costing you not only money but aggravation, right?" Then the DM addresses the aggravation by offering a solution: "If I could offer you a solution and take away that aggravation for all of your deliveries, such that you and your subcontractor are not always at odds with one another, would you be interested?" The customer responds, "Well, hell yeah, I would be interested." By this time, the customer has pretty much signed on the dotted line, and the DM moves into the pricing for the desired services.

HACK 30 >>>>>>>>>>>>>>>>>>>>>>>>>>>>>>>>>>>>

Don't Cut-to-the-Chase (Big Four "Moves")

It all started with an email that I sent to a staff member in our executive center prior to a big program. Tired from the various frustrations of the day, I quickly tried to ready myself for the following day by speed-reading my overflowing inbox and banging out quick replies. In one particular email, I summarized a "countdown list" for the executive course launch the following morning, and sent it to Linda, the staff member in charge. In hindsight, my email to Linda was not just telegraphic, but looked like a strange version of Morse code: "yes, fine but need more copies by class AM"; "put mat on desk 1 hour to program start," etc.

The following day, I trotted into the classroom and Linda approached me carrying the requested materials for the teaching session. She stood there with a stiff posture and a red, strained-looking face. I dumbly said, "Hi," and apparently that was the last straw. She threw my classroom materials onto the floor and stalked out. Stupefied, I ran after her and asked for an explanation, but that only seemed to add more gasoline to the fire. Linda held a printed copy of my email, which she ceremoniously ripped up in front me, announcing, "I want nothing more to do with you." And walked away.

Now, here's the thing: I had no idea what she was talking about. No idea what I'd done wrong. I bent down, picked up the pieces, and reread my email. Harmless, I thought. What was the problem?

Baffled, I decided to practice what I preach and did a "perspective-taking hack." I imagined that I was a subordinate and had received an email like mine from a high-ranking superior (my dean, the provost, or the university president). All of a sudden my terse words took on new meaning: What seemed like a simple countdown summary now appeared to be a command-and-control directive issued by a heartless autocrat. Clearly, this was not my intent. I was simply trying to save us both time! I also noticed that there were no pleasantries in my email. Rather, it was literally a bulleted to-do list. Zero human factor! To my dismay, I realized upon looking through my "sent mail" to Linda that I'd been doing this for some time, and that had led her, finally, to blow a gasket and confront me.

A few days later, I asked for a personal meeting with Linda and said I was sorry. I did not try to justify or explain my actions. I simply said, "I value the work that you do and I'm very upset that I insulted you. I apologize." She accepted my apology perfunctorily, but was clearly still upset. It made sense: I was the one who needed to change. I made a point from then on to: (1) never send emails that were hastily written, and (2) to always include a greeting and a sign-off.

About six months later, Linda walked up to me and said she was ready to hit the reset button and move on. I beamed and said, "I feel the same way," and extended my hand. She reached out to hug me and we both let out a sigh of relief. In general, I've worked hard to develop email best practices including the ones above. In addition to those, I am careful to reread all emails to staff before I hit the "send" button. Also, I never send emails at night—figuring my alertness is at a low. I begin and end every email with a heartfelt pleasantry: "I'm looking forward to working with you . . . ," "Warmly . . . ," "Appreciatively . . . ," etc.

After that fateful experience with Linda, I reflected on why some email interactions seemed more difficult to manage than others. I noticed that when there was a *power differential* between the parties involved, the words can take on an unintended meaning.

Research by Stanford Business School professor Rod Kramer and colleagues sheds insight on the very different points of view held by those with power (in the hasty email situation, that was me) and those without power (in this situation, that was the staff member).[52] Kramer found that when people have power in a social-organizational situation, they are effectively operating on auto-pilot, lacking in self-awareness, with little understanding of the social or situational context around them. Those without power, however, are on hyper-alert, carefully monitoring the situation and deconstructing each interaction in an attempt to find meaning and understand cause and effect.

Kramer shared his own story to illustrate this reality, a narrative with themes like my story about Linda. At Stanford, when he stepped into an elevator filled with agitated PhD students concerned about their uncertain status in the doctoral program, the professor was thinking only about his lecture later that afternoon. Kramer mumbled a few words to the students, who knew that he was among those who could decide their fate. Later, Kramer couldn't recall when he was in the elevator, much less who else was there. However, the PhD students, when he asked them about it later, accurately recalled the exact time of day, the particular suit Kramer wore, and how his averted eyes surely meant that they would not in fact be admitted to candidacy. Kramer learned this only after starting a research project on how powerful people often have lower situational awareness than do those who have significantly less power, like his PhD students did. The point: People in power are much less aware of the environment, because they don't have to be. Conversely, people who lack organizational power observe and dissect every move and gesture (or lack thereof) of those on top, to understand their relative position and security in the hierarchy. This is important for those with power to keep in mind, as I'd failed to in my situation with Linda the staff member.

Professor Deborah Gruenfeld and colleagues examined how powerful and less powerful people behave at social events, such as cocktail parties.[53] Powerful people eat more, and eat messier food, for example, all with a reckless abandon. Meanwhile, those lacking in power carefully choose less messy foods and self-monitor their eating behavior more closely.

An in-depth study of business letters exchanged via fax between a Brazilian company and two European companies provided insight into the language that leads to trust rather than emphasizing power imbalances or other issues.[54] Turns out four main "moves" defined and structured the business letters: Move 1: Establishing the negotiation chain; Move 2: Providing information and answers; Move 3: Requesting information and action; and Move 4: Ending. The key here is that Moves 1 and 2 *frame* the other two moves, which together form the key content. However, if one simply jumps into the content (ignoring Move 1 and Move 4), this is not likely to lead to success. In my hastily written email to Linda, I went straight to Move 3 (making a request) and skipped all the others—which led to the negative outcome.

Opening moves were also pivotal in a study of domestic and international email negotiations.[55] One of the most important determinants of successful e-negotiations was the parties' up-front stated intentions of pursuing a mutually beneficial outcome. So this entire section is about framing communications in a positive way, resisting the temptation to simply cut to the chase, which has proven to lead to much worse outcomes.

HACK 31 >>>>>>>>>>>>>>>>>>>>>>>>>>>>>>>>>>>>

I'm Sorry About the Weather

Sometimes, despite our best intentions, interactions—particularly those that involve differences of opinion and conflict—go south. The question is how to break out of the doom-loop and effectively hit the reset button once you realize that the interaction is deteriorating.

One of the most powerful ways to hit the reset button is to apologize. Now, keep in mind there are two key *types* of apologies: the *routine* apology (e.g., "I'm sorry to bother you") and the *heartfelt* apology ("I am sorry that I was short-tempered on the conference call yesterday").[56] Heartfelt apologies are particularly impactful when they are sincere and immediate; you don't want the other party stewing and waiting a long time to hear from you. What about "routine" apologies? Whereas it might seem that routine or superfluous apologies (e.g., "I'm sorry about the rain") would have little or no positive impact, that's not the case! Routine apologies increase trust in the apologizer.[57] Why? Issuing a superfluous apology demonstrates empathic concern for the "victim" and increases their trust and goodwill toward the apologizer.

Another study examined apologies in business emails, and found that acceptance of apologies in natural emails is not that common, except for very serious offenses.[58] Why? Acceptance of apologies confirms that an offense has actually taken place. One business publication provided a "template" for writing heartfelt apologies and noted that something like the following is nearly ideal:[59] I wholeheartedly agree!

Hi Zoe,

Hope you're doing well. I just wanted to take a minute and apologize for forwarding the most recent draft of our research to the client before you'd weighed in. I thought I was being proactive, but I realize that I should have checked with you first. I apologize sincerely, and I've instituted an online approvals and review process with our communications and IR teams so that it won't happen again. Is there anything else I can do to help get things back on track? I'd be happy to discuss at your convenience.

Sincerely,
Taylor

To be sure, parties in conflict may attempt to build trust and empathy via apology, but sometimes it can be rejected or dismissed by the other party. Empathy is a joint interactive effort in which people verify, confirm, and reconfirm the legitimacy of their experiences, interests, and needs. The key hack is to realize that when your attempts at empathy are rejected, this is often just reflective of a phase in the process, not a break-down.[60] So keep trying, with as heartfelt communications as possible.

HACK 32 >>>>>>>>>>>>>>>>>>>>>>>>>>>>>>>>>>>>>>

Lying and Lie Detection

One empirical observation from studies of online interaction is that people are more likely to lie, cheat, and deceive when communicating virtually, rather than face-to-face, in line with our earlier discussions.[61] To be sure, this is highly risky behavior, given that anything sent virtually leaves a permanent record. So why do people seem to forget this and send what appear to be regrettable messages via the internet? Apparently, when people communicate face-to-face, an area of the brain is activated that, well, makes us more human and empathic and induces us to be truthful. When we are not face-to-face, we lack the social signals that stimulate that part of the brain, and many of us behave in a less ethical fashion.

One study used a diary method to track deception, asking participants to record all of their social interactions, including lies, for seven days.[62] What happened? In this investigation, participants lied most on the telephone and least in email. Notice that this pattern is the opposite of what was found in the previously mentioned study, so it appears that the incidence of lying virtually is extremely context-dependent. Lying rates in face-to-face and instant messaging interactions were approximately equal. This pattern of results suggests that the design features of communication technologies, such as synchronicity, recordability, and co-presence, affect lying behavior.

Given that there is nearly always temptation to use deception in a negotiation, most people are interested in detecting such behavior, so as to prevent economic loss. This is hard to do because liars (and other deceptive people) are motivated to avoid being caught, and thus work to create an impression that promotes trust. So, how do you detect lying? It's very difficult! Even skilled professionals, such as law enforcement and customs inspectors, often perform at chance level with lie-detection.[63] If you have several years to train with world-class communication experts like Dr. Paul Ekman, you can probably improve your lie-detection skills.[64] But most of us can't take several years off to get a PhD in communication theory. So guess what? That's right: we need a hack!

In this case, the answer may be all in the words. Literally, the number of words. One study examined text-based conversations between "liars" and their conversational partners in truthful and deceptive communication.[65] Overall, liars produced more words and more sensory types of words (e.g., "I *see* what you are getting at" and "*touching* on that point, I have some *thoughts* about . . ." and the like) and used more other-oriented pronouns (e.g., "you") when lying.

Most lie-detection techniques rely on the analysis of nonverbal behavior, such as facial expression and paralinguistic cues. What about detecting lies in virtual modes of communication such as text and email, where there are no nonverbal cues? Deception theory suggests that deceptive writing is characterized by reduced frequency of first-person pronouns and exclusive words, and elevated frequency of negative emotion words and action verbs. One investigation applied this model of deception to the Enron (energy business found guilty of massive fraud) email dataset.[66] When the Enron emails were ranked by how well they fit the profile of deception (i.e., reduced first-person pronouns and exclusive words, more negative emotion words and action verbs), the emails fitting that pattern were more likely to include deceptive communications; other emails that were ranked highly using these frequency counts also indicated organizational dysfunctions such as improper communication of information.

HACK 33 >>>>>>>>>>>>>>>>>>>>>>>>>>>>>>>>>>>>

Put Pride Aside

As we've established, people behave differently when they are not face-to-face. They are more negative and, often, more presumptuous, conveying the impression that they are entitled and not easy to work with. This is a problem because excessive pride or hubris harms our ability to locate the sweet spot in any kind of negotiation. If we are unwittingly conveying negative impressions in non-face-to-face interactions, we need a wake-up call!

Excessive pride may blind us to finding sweet spots. Why? Whether we realize it or not, people quickly develop impressions of our personalities on the basis of very limited information. In fact, some research studies suggest we develop lasting impressions of people within minutes—sometimes seconds!—of meeting them![67] This means that within minutes or seconds of composing and sending an email to someone, the recipient is already forming a character sketch of your personality!

Several research investigations have examined emails and other written communication of leaders as windows into their personality. For example, the "dark personality" traits—narcissism, Machiavellianism (allowing the ends always to justify the means), and hubris—can be measured by examining writing styles. In this context, some have speculated that the banking crisis of 2008 was caused partly by CEO hubris. One study examined CEO letters to shareholders of a single bank over ten years for evidence of personality traits including narcissism, hubris, overconfidence, and CEO attribution (i.e., how leaders explain good and bad events).[68] Over half of the CEOs' sentences contained "narcissistic-speak." And, in 45 percent of the narcissistic-speak sentences, there were three more symptoms of hubris—signifying what is known as "extreme hubristic" behavior.[69] The symptoms: very little "bad news" was communicated; more than half of the "good news" was attributed to the CEO; and all the bad news was attributed externally. The longer the CEO served, the more hubris the researchers found in the writing!

It's easy to see how hubristic communication can damage negotiations and other interactions. So, what's the put-pride-aside hack? Look carefully at your important written communications before sending these out. Avoid using the royal "we" (using "we" when you mean to say "I") and don't speak in third-person about yourself. Ideally, have a peer read your critical communications carefully to look for boastful, gloating, arrogant, or patronizing statements. Also, avoid reckless and impulsive language. As an example, consider the case of J.D., an executive student and client, the director of portfolio management in a large pharmaceutical firm. J.D. was involved in a negotiation with a biotech company partner in the design of a clinical trial. Partway through, J.D. shared with me a draft of an email he intended to send to the "opposing party": *After consideration of multiple study designs to achieve a robust, statistically significant endpoint to drive a "go/no-go" decision, we are in agreement on the following design.*

I told J.D. that the communication had all three markers of hubris: his use of "we," his arrogant assumption that his design was the *only* one, and his thinly veiled threat of walking away—the "no go" part (impulsive language). With considerable prodding from me, J.D. ultimately revised his email to read: *I'm happy to report that my team and I considered a number of study designs with the goal of obtaining clear findings. There is consensus on one particular design for the trial. I'm very keen to hear what your thoughts are on the design [below].* J.D. reported to me that the biotech partner was receptive to the proposed design and they moved forward in the partnership, reaching a sweet spot deal!

*   *   *

Given the ubiquity of e-communication, we must be proactive about cultivating and enhancing our communication style. Merely relying on "gut instinct" or what works well in our face-to-face encounters may be misinterpreted by our e-communication recipient. People who rely on auto-pilot to compose and reply to emails, texts, and phone messages are likely to fall prey to one of the e-communication whammies, with poor outcomes. Use the ideas here to avoid that.

CHAPTER EIGHT

Putting It All Together

WE'VE COVERED A LOT OF GROUND SO FAR AND DISCUSSED a smorgasbord of "hacks" to find the sweet spot in personal, business, and virtual life. If you are like many of my students, who have demanding jobs, busy families, and an overcommitted schedule, you are probably feeling overwhelmed. How on Earth can you start to put these ideas into real action? Let's face it: It's one thing to read about something; it's quite another to put it into practice.

By now you probably know what that means: We need action hacks! Think of action hacks as hacks for hacks! You'll find the full set of action hacks in the pages that follow.

*   *   *

HACK 34 >>>>>>>>>>>>>>>>>>>>>>>>>>>>>>>>>>>>>

Multivitamin

The multivitamin action hack is my personal favorite for just about everything in my life, from making the bed, to doing "core exercises" and journaling. The simple idea is that if you want to make something a habit, you need to do it once per day, no matter what. You can pick the time and the place but it needs to happen each day, every day! For example, you can't skip a given activity and say, "I will do double-duty tomorrow." For me, this means that I'm doing "core" exercises right before bed, or journaling while I'm waiting for the train. It's not about making it perfect, but making a good-faith attempt.

The good news is that you can use nearly any daily situation as a test-bed for trying one of the sweet spot hacks in this book. For example, I found myself in a tough spot when I served on an educational design committee with several other faculty that included full, associate, and clinical professors. One of the committee members was an adjunct lecturer, whose role I understood was to "provide assistance and support." So I asked him to prepare reports, collect information, and schedule meetings. He provided the reports and information, but fell short when it came to scheduling the meetings. After about two or three months of my making repeated requests for meetings that he didn't fulfill, we were both frustrated. So, I tried a perspective-taking hack with the goal of learning more about how he saw his role on the team. As noted above, I had considered him a support person who provides information and support for the design team members. However, he saw his role quite differently: He did not see himself as just providing assistance, but rather as a substantive contributor to the design team. During a one-on-one meeting, I asked him point blank why the meetings were never scheduled. He frowned and said that he saw that task as "beneath" him, something that he should not be doing. This gave me an idea. "So," I said, "if I found someone—perhaps even myself—who would do the work of scheduling meetings, would you be willing to provide the reports and information for those meetings?" This did the trick. He said that arrangement would make him much happier. From that point on, we worked well together.

HACK 35 >>>>>>>>>>>>>>>>>>>>>>>>>>>>>>>>>>>>>

Route 66

It takes about sixty-six days (a little over two months) for a given behavior to become a habit. By habit, we mean that a behavior becomes a reasonably permanent part of your response hierarchy. Phillippa Lally is a health psychologist who examined the habits of ninety-six people over a twelve-week period.[1] Each person chose one new habit for the twelve-week study and reported daily whether they performed the behavior and how "automatic" it felt. Some people chose simple habits like "drinking a bottle of water with lunch." Others chose more difficult tasks like "running for fifteen minutes before dinner." It took anywhere from eighteen days to 254 days for people to form a new habit, meaning they performed the behavior automatically, with little thought; sixty-six days was the average. Most important is that if you miss one day, it will not materially affect the habit-formation process. So give each hack at least sixty-six days to become part of your DNA!

In my case, I needed to break a habit and replace it with a new, effective hack. Prior to a few years ago, I had a (bad) habit of responding immediately to emails, presumably out of a compulsive need to empty my inbox. I was also sending emails late in the evening, again to stay on top of things. Unfortunately, this meant that two undesirable things were happening. On more than one occasion, I sent the email to the wrong person (in one case intended for Taryn T. but went to a different Taryn). This was embarrassing. "Thank goodness I wasn't planning a murder!" I offered weakly when the receiving party pointed out my mistake. A more serious problem was that my emails sometimes appeared too harsh or defensive, such as when I was responding to a problem or denying a request. So I adopted a hack of never sending an email after 6:00 p.m. that was in any way negative; instead I would compose a message, place it in my "draft" folder, sleep on it, and invariably edit it the next morning with fresh eyes.

Blame It on "TML"

As you probably can tell, I come on strong in my writing style; the same goes for my teaching. My students have accused me of "getting right up in their face" when it comes to my classroom teaching and discussions of conflict, collaboration, and negotiation skills. As a female, I know that I defy a lot of stereotypes about being demure, soft-spoken, and diplomatic. So, I created a hack that I use in the classroom: I essentially disarm myself by referring to myself as the "tall mean lady" or "TML." When I refer to myself as the TML, the class usually laughs because I've articulated what they've all been thinking (but don't dare say). So, once we all know that I'm going to use a confrontational style that I own—and that it's not personal—the classroom discussion goes much better.

How could this hack work for you? In two ways. First, if anyone starts to accuse you of being meddlesome, or a conflict-skills-know-it all, just create your own nickname. "Yep, I'm trying to help everyone I know find the sweet spot whether they like it or not! Call me 'doctor know-it-all'!" Second, you can always blame me! As in, "I made a personal commitment to put some of what I've been reading in this negotiation book into action."

HACK 37 ›››››››››››››››››››››››››››››››››››

Elevator Pitch

One hack I admit to using (and benefiting from) is to casually start up a dinner conversation with people by mentioning a research study. With a lot of people, this leads to an immediate eye-roll and glancing at their iPhone, so I try to make it as punchy and interesting as possible, hoping for some kind of reaction. "Did you hear that when people fall silent during a discussion and don't say anything for about twenty seconds, they often come up with a win-win solution?" (might be good with a teenager). "I keep thinking about this research on mirroring body language. As someone who works in sales, what do you think?" (might be good with a salesperson). The key, of course, in mentioning these one-liners, is to learn how to quickly introduce one of the sweet spot hacks—almost in an elevator pitch type way—and then engage the other person in a discussion. No doubt they will pepper you with questions, and that's your way of learning to explain and articulate the hack.

One of my students used the elevator pitch hack to land herself a job offer. She was in the middle of a formal interview with a firm when a loud conflict erupted in an adjacent room. The interviewer apologized for the "heated discussion" down the hall: "Those are two of our most strong-willed partners in the firm and they don't always see eye to eye." Hearing this, my student thoughtfully brought up the "hot-warm-cold" hack and told a story of how she managed to resolve a highly emotional conflict simulation by moving away from "accept-reject" conversations to "hot-warm-cold." The discussion then pivoted to win-win solutions and their value in partner-client relationships. She walked out of the interview with a job offer in hand!

Teach One

The idea of the "teach one" hack is to help someone else with their own conflict or negotiation situation. Many of us work with colleagues who are not shy about sharing their own "people problems." I often challenge myself to not simply commiserate with anyone who brings a "people problem" my way (e.g., "Yes, the world is full of jerks"), but rather to gently put the focus on them (e.g., "You know, usually there are two legitimate sides to a conflict. I wonder what the other person is saying right now to their coworker about you?"). I try not to be confrontational but to convey something like, "Tell me more about your situation. I'm not a licensed clinician, but I have spent some time reading about best-practice hacks for conflict in relationships and the workplace and I would love to see if any of them might help in this situation."

In one case, Theresa, a manager-student in an evening MBA program, told me about a particularly stressful workplace conflict regarding a senior leader, Ron, who in her mind was deliberately working to derail her career. "Why would that be his motivation?" I asked. "Well, the clients prefer to work with me and that is intimidating for him, so he tries to undermine me in client meetings," she responded. Theresa's explanation reminded me of my work with Professor Tanya Menon on threat immunity, in which people think they threaten others but not vice-versa. In this situation, I was unlikely to get Ron's side of the story, so we needed to devise a hack that could work. I asked Theresa to tell me about an upcoming meeting with the client, and then we went to work devising how she could use several hacks if needed: *I'm not angry, I'm disappointed, get your 'we' on*, and the *skin in the game* hacks. Then, if Ron attempted to undermine her in the meeting, instead of attacking him on the spot, Theresa would express disappointment and suggest that they put the different strategies to the test. Like this: *"You can see that we, as the client team, have strong differences of opinion about your business challenges. We like to consider different approaches before settling on one. We are a spirited bunch, but we are aligned on fully addressing your needs, and given that we are data-driven, we have some ideas on how to test the effectiveness of our interventions."*

It turned out that Ron did attempt to undermine Theresa in the next client meeting, by suggesting that the research she had conducted was "futile and worthless." Theresa brilliantly kept her cool and then proposed the *skin in the game* hack, offering to do a beta test of the likely effectiveness of two interventions. The client loved the evidence-based approach and it helped Theresa increase her credibility, while probably making Ron think twice about future efforts to undermine her.

Bachelor in Paradise

One of my many vices is watching reality TV shows. I know that as an allegedly "distinguished" professor I'm supposed to say that I'm above TV and that I spend my spare time reading intellectual books and arcane research reports. Actually, nothing could be further from the truth. To make matters worse, I tend to be drawn toward TV shows that contain a lot of (probably fake) emotion. I'm gullible enough to be drawn in. One of my favorite shows is *Bachelor* (and *Bachelorette*) *in Paradise*. The premise is simple: A single male (or female) is put on an island with a lot of available women (men) and after several months of filming and going on dates he (she) chooses one. Along the way, several relationships crop up and take various turns and twists. Naturally, drama, conflict, misunderstanding, and he-said/she-said situations abound.

This is where the hack comes in. When I see a couple on the show that is experiencing some kind of relationship stress, I try to think of a hack that could work. "Don't get angry at her, dude! Show disappointment!" Or, "Don't say you've lost trust in him. Tell him that you are 'suspicious'!" And, "Stop using the word 'I' when you talk about your relationship! Start using the word 'we'!"

Okay. No doubt you've seen right through me. I justify watching juvenile TV shows under the guise of "I'm doing observational research." What I can tell you is if you try watching a show like my guilty pleasure you'll quickly learn that you don't need to reach for this book or your notes to find a relationship sweet spot hack, given all the practice the show will give you. They will be top of mind!

By the way, before you lose all faith in me, I have a few "business-context" shows that I essentially do the same hack with. While writing this book, I've been doing some "evening research" with the shows *Succession* (HBO) and *Billions* (Showtime). These shows put characters in a number of tricky business situations where many of our workplace hacks could come in quite handy!

HACK 40 >>>>>>>>>>>>>>>>>>>>>>>>>>>>>>>>>>>>>

Let's Try Something Different

One of the things that I have observed about conflict, whether at home or in the workplace, is that it is often recurrent, meaning that couples tend to argue about similar things and co-workers often continue to lock horns about the same issues. This is usually because the conflict is unresolved and tends to reemerge. When the conflict reemerges, people pick up "old scripts" and essentially play out the same lines. This of course can be very frustrating for all the parties involved.

One way to potentially break out of this pattern is to suggest putting down the old script by proposing, "Let's try something different." This suggestion will no doubt be met with skepticism: "What exactly do you have in mind?" or even "I'm not going to agree to your terms if that's what you're suggesting!" The key is to tell the other person that you see yourselves caught up in a lose-lose cycle and that you have played a part in this and want ideally to find a win-win or sweet spot solution so that both of you can move forward. Assuming the other party agrees that they would like to move forward, you can introduce a suggestion (based on a sweet spot hack).

One clever executive student of mine tried this in a workplace conflict when a meeting with a peer leader got particularly heated. He suggested the "write on the wall hack," often used for group situations; but in this case, he remembered the visual contact and testosterone study I had mentioned, and promised the opponent that if they did not see some progress they could "return to insulting one another!"

HACK 41 >>>>>>>>>>>>>>>>>>>>>>>>>>>>>>>>>>>>

Noah's Ark Method

In my teaching I make extensive use of experiential learning—because I know that when people engage in a real-life-like business simulation (rather than just passively reading a case), they learn much more. However, the challenge is ensuring that the business simulation used in a classroom or training session will lead to best practices in real business situations.

I quickly became obsessed with this challenge—something that my colleagues and I called "the knowledge transfer" problem.[2] To our horror, we found that managers often don't use the best practices they've learned in class in subsequent business situations. This observation was heartbreaking for us, because it indicated that managers have a highly effective toolkit, but they don't use it! This unfortunate situation is called the *inert knowledge problem*—illustrated by the student who laments, "I knew the answer, but I couldn't think of it during the exam!"[3] Given that common business situations are in essence real-life "final exams," how can we make knowledge more portable, usable, and accessible—not just for businesspeople but for anyone seeking the sweet spot in work and life? We need a hack!

My colleagues and I have conducted dozens of experiments on the inert knowledge problem, emerging with a hack I call the "Noah's Ark Method," which I teach regularly. Here's how it works: When attempting to learn a new skill, strategy, or tactic, don't just read one business case or example of the skill in action—read two or more. Just as Noah put two of every animal on the ark for his biblical journey, the skilled manager needs to make sure that they study at least two examples of every best practice. Why? When we read a business case (or hear an example) that contains a key learning point, the material contains both *superficial* information and *substantive* information. Ideally, we need to retain the substantive information and not get bogged down by superficial information. By analyzing two or more cases or examples that make the same substantive point (but may contain very different superficial details), we are more likely to remember the substantive knowledge. The hack is to figure out how to keep your eye on the forest and not get distracted by the single trees within it.

In my research, I tested this tree-forest idea by encouraging people to *generalize* across multiple divergent scenario examples. We found that when we suggested that people read a number of case examples and generalize across them, they improved their learning and engaged in greater subsequent knowledge transfer to new situations.[4] For example, managers who were asked *broad questions* about a negotiation scenario from an unfamiliar industry (e.g., "How might this strategy relate to your own business negotiations?") were more open-minded than managers asked *narrow questions* about a scenario from a familiar industry (e.g., "What is going on in this situation?"). Openness, in turn, led to their successfully applying the key learning point in the scenario to resolve a subsequent *in vivo* negotiation scenario.

That means that when managers are exposed only to negotiation scenarios in their own industry, they are less able to bring key insights to subsequent, novel situations. In the research, both the case study familiarity intervention and the type of question had a significant impact on learning. And, when the two interventions were combined, such that managers were exposed to a negotiation strategy in an unfamiliar industry *and* asked broadening questions, this produced a more than threefold improvement compared to their baseline performance! Stated in terms of financial returns, managers who read case studies that exposed them to an unfamiliar industry and were asked broad questions (e.g., "How might this apply in your industry?") ultimately crafted negotiation deals in a new situation that generated over $1 million more in profit. They were nearly three times more likely to find the sweet spot than people who, well, "stuck to the knitting" of their own industry; the latter group could not see the forest, only the trees.

Remember: the Noah's Ark Method and all the other hacks in this book apply not only to business situations but broader life, too. In this case, the idea is to use learning from multiple examples and experiences to sharpen key sweet spot–finding skills, whether at work, in your relationships, or any other kind of interaction. The right kind of learning and practice makes perfect.

In closing, keep in mind that not all of your attempts to find the sweet spot in your personal, workplace, and online conflicts will meet with success. For example, Stephanie, an executive student of mine, called me, really frustrated with her job, in particular the opaqueness of her company's compensation system: "Each time we get a new client, there is a big fight for how to divide the revenues—there's no transparent system and I feel that I'm being taken advantage of!" So Stephanie tried implementing a brainwriting hack wherein each member of the client team proposed a revenue-sharing plan that would serve as a transparent model going forward. Stephanie led a great brainwriting session and managed to resolve the conflict related to the most recent new client, but she was not successful in getting the team to agree on a standard revenue-sharing system going forward. She ultimately realized she would continue to be frustrated (and underpaid), given the lack of clarity and responsiveness, so she took a new job outside the company. "They just didn't share my values," she said. While Stephanie couldn't resolve the core conflict at her old company, she "got to a better place in life much more quickly," as she said, because she raised the issue in the first place and tested her firm's values.

Conflict, disputes, misunderstandings, and negotiations are all opportunities to find sweet spots in life and work, both in the real and virtual worlds. Our fears and hesitations about coming to the table with people who don't see our point of view are natural responses we can overcome when we implement strategies to find the sweet spot.

I hope you feel motivated to apply the strategies here to a wide range of life situations. I'm confident you'll be glad you did.

Afterword

ON JULY 14, 2018, A SATURDAY, I WAS ON AN EASY EARLY
morning bike ride up a path with my friend Dany. What I did
not see until it was too late was a pedestrian with a large backpack, earbuds in place, iPhone in hand, approaching us on the
left. I quickly moved right, but his backpack hit my handle-
bar. My bike stopped instantly, and I went down. Hard. I felt
the back of my helmet hit the asphalt. I raised myself to hands
and knees, struggling to stand. "Are you okay?" Dany asked,
holding a hand out. "I don't know," I said, standing now.
"Let's walk it off," she suggested. But I couldn't: my right leg
wouldn't move. After fifteen minutes of standing and not
moving, I called 911, seeing no other option.

Dany stayed with the bikes and I got an ambulance ride to
the ER. Once there, I tried to calm myself down. I had a sharp

pain near my groin. I started googling "groin strain" and "groin tear" while waiting to be seen. Would I be able to complete my four-hour ride on Sunday, I wondered.

The attending doctor explained he was not an orthopedic guy. He wanted to rule out a broken femur, and pressed around that area. "You'd be screaming in pain if you had a broken femur," he said. "But you're not. Still, we've got to X-ray you."

Getting onto the X-ray table was clumsy and painful. Then, a really long wait. That gave me time for more iPhone research. I started making mental lists of worst-case scenarios to calm myself down. My husband was out of town. My son and teenage daughter were asleep at home; only my son knew how to drive.

When the attending doctor returned after forty-five minutes, he avoided eye contact. That's when I knew it was bad news. "There are fractures," he said quietly. I felt tears forming. He pointed to the X-rays and directed me to look at the image of my right pelvis. "Fractures in two places." Pubis Ramus fractures. My hopes of riding the next day were gone. My mind leaped forward to the worst possible scenarios. "Surgery?" I asked "Immobility?" The doctor didn't have any answers. He wanted me to see an orthopedic surgeon within the next forty-eight hours.

I was freezing in my torn, sweaty cycling jersey and bike shorts. All I wanted was to get out of there. I wanted a warm shower and my own bed. But the doctor said, "I can't let you leave. It's not safe."

"What do I need to do in order to leave?" I asked.

"Show me that you can walk around the ER."

"How far?" I negotiated.

"All the way down the hall."

"Can I cling to a wall?"

"No."

"What about crutches?"

"No. I don't think so . . . too unstable."

Finally, I negotiated a deal wherein I could be released if I demonstrated that I could move by using a walker, which I did. I called my sleeping son. No answer. "Can I take an Uber?" I asked. The doctor shook his head. So I called my daughter, who woke my son to pick me up.

The rest of the weekend was hell. I slept belly up on an icepack, pillow shoved under my right leg, playing music all night to stop my racing mind.

The following Monday I received the first piece of good news: I would not require surgery. However, it would be six to eight weeks before I could ride a bike outside. No big deal, right?

Wrong. For the past twelve years, cycling had become my identity. I started "riding" in 2006, "training" in 2007, and "racing" in 2008. I trained like a cyborg and won the Masters National Time Trial championship in 2008. In 2010, I set my sights higher and won the Masters World Championship. I was the Illinois State Time Trial Champion for eight years. I owned nine bikes and trained fifteen hours a week. It was an indelible part of me.

I quickly spiraled down mentally. Seeing my bikes stabled in the garage, office, and house caused me to weep uncontrollably. I knew how quickly my aerobic fitness would deteriorate, along with my mental health, which was really an extension of my cycling.

My husband and daughter told me to find a way to channel all the energy, training time, and dedication that I normally put into cycling into something else. But I couldn't imagine what that might be, given how much cycling meant to me.

I began to think about who I was before I discovered cycling—yes, such a time existed. One morning I awoke and thought about the long day ahead that would *not* involve putting on bike shorts and rolling out of my garage. In that moment, I envisioned writing a new book about finding "win-win" solutions to problems that seem intractable and frustrating.

I decided to treat the writing project like a training plan. I would pick a starting time and specific length of time that I would write each day. Interval training. I would set some simple goals. The first day was frustrating. I was depressed. *Just put some words on a page*, I told myself. Instead of forcing it, I started imagining being in the classroom. I thought about some of my favorite students and the conversations that we'd had. The words began to flow.

As the words flowed faster, my mood lifted. On day ten, I attempted to sit on my bike—mounted firmly and securely to a "trainer" in my office. I pedaled easily for thirty minutes. And I wrote for thirty minutes. Each day, I increased the amount of time that I spent on the book and the bike.

I don't know if it was the book that allowed me to get back on the bike or the bike that allowed me to write the book. The book and bike were my win-win in what seemed to be a horribly painful lose-lose situation.

This book, the product of that difficult period and a symbol of overcoming life's biggest challenges, is dedicated to all the people who I care about and who have helped me find the sweet spot in very dark moments.

Notes

CHAPTER ONE

1. Simon, H. A. (1955). A behavioral model of rational choice. *Quarterly Journal of Economics, 69*, 99–118.
2. Pruitt, D. G., & Rubin, J. Z. (1986). *Social conflict: Escalation, stalemate and settlement*. Random House.
3. Heath, C. (1999). On the social psychology of agency relationships: Lay theories of motivation overemphasize extrinsic incentives. *Organizational Behavior and Human Decision Processes, 78*(1), 25–62.
4. Kelley, H. H., & Stahelski, A. J. (1970). Social interaction basis of cooperators' and competitors' beliefs about others. *Journal of Personality and Social Psychology, 16*(1), 66.
5. Thompson, L. (1995). The impact of minimum goals and aspirations on judgments of success in negotiations. *Group Decision and Negotiation, 4*(6), 513–524.
6. Thompson, L., Valley, K. L., & Kramer, R. M. (1995). The bittersweet feeling of success: An examination of social per-

ception in negotiation. *Journal of Experimental Social Psychology, 31*(6), 467–492.

7. Curhan, J. R., Elfenbein, H. A., & Xu, H. (2006). What do people value when they negotiate? Mapping the domain of subjective value in negotiation. *Journal of Personality and Social Psychology, 91*(3), 493–512.

8. Follett, M. (1930). *Creative experience*. Longmans, Green and Co.; Graham, P. (1994). *Mary Parker Follett: Prophet of management—A celebration of writings from the 1920s*. Harvard Business School Press.

9. Yaffe-Bellany, D. (2019, July 3). Drink a pint, waste less food. *New York Times*. nytimes.com

10. Nadler, J., Thompson, L., & Boven, L. V. (2003). Learning negotiation skills: Four models of knowledge creation and transfer. *Management Science, 49*(4), 529–540.

11. Thompson, L., & Hastie, R. (1990). Social perception in negotiation. *Organizational Behavior and Human Decision Processes, 47*(1), 98–123.

12. Thompson, L., & Hrebec, D. (1996). Lose–lose agreements in interdependent decision making. *Psychological Bulletin, 120*(3), 396.

CHAPTER TWO

1. Nash, J. (1950). The bargaining problem. *Econometrica, 18*, 155–162.

2. Howard, R., Grazer, B. (Producers), & Howard, R. (Director). (2001). *A beautiful mind*. United States: Universal Pictures.

3. Pareto, V. (1935). *The Mind and society* [Trattato Di Sociologia Generale], Harcourt, Brace and Company.

4. Formally, a given option, x, is a member of the Pareto frontier if and only if, no option y exists such that y is preferred to x by at least one party and is at least as good as x for the other party.

CHAPTER THREE

1. Bazerman, M. H., & Neale, M. A. (1983). Heuristics in negotiation: Limitations to effective dispute resolution. In M. Bazerman & R. Lewicki (eds.), *Negotiating in organizations* (pp. 51–67). Sage Publications; Thompson, L., & Hastie, R. (1990). Social perception in negotiation. *Organizational Behavior and Human Decision Processes, 47*(1), 98–123.
2. O'Connor, K. M., & Adams, A. A. (1999). What novices think about negotiation: A content analysis of scripts. *Negotiation Journal, 15*(2), 135–148.
3. Thompson, L., & Hastie, R. (1990). Social perception in negotiation. *Organizational Behavior and Human Decision Processes, 47*(1), 98–123.
4. Thompson, L. (1991). Information exchange in negotiation. *Journal of Experimental Social Psychology, 27*(2), 161–179.
5. Thompson, L. (1990). An examination of naïve and experienced negotiators. *Journal of Personality and Social Psychology, 59*(1), 82–90; Thompson, L. (1990). The influence of experience on negotiation performance. *Journal of Experimental Social Psychology, 26*(6), 528–544.
6. Thompson, L., & DeHarpport, T. (1994). Social judgment, feedback, and interpersonal learning in negotiation. *Organizational Behavior and Human Decision Processes, 58*(3), 327–345.
7. Liu, W., Liu, L.A., & Zhang, J-D. (2016). How to dissolve fixed-pie bias in negotiation? Social antecedents and the mediating effect of mental-model adjustment. *Journal of Organizational Behavior, 37*(1), 85–107.
8. Deutsch, M. (1973). *The resolution of conflict.* Yale University Press.

CHAPTER FOUR

1. Kray, L. J., & Haselhuhn, M. P. (2007). Implicit negotiation beliefs and performance: Experimental and longitudinal evidence. *Journal of Personality and Social Psychology, 93*(1), 49–64.

2. Wong, E. M., Haselhuhn, M. P., & Kray, L. J. (2012). Improving the future by considering the past: The impact of upward counterfactual reflection and implicit beliefs on negotiation performance. *Journal of Experimental Social Psychology, 48*(1), 403–406.

3. Van Boven, L., & Thompson, L. (2003). A look into the mind of the negotiator: Mental models in negotiation. *Group Processes & Intergroup Relations, 6*(4), 387–404.

4. Nadler, J., Thompson, L., & Boven, L. V. (2003). Learning negotiation skills: Four models of knowledge creation and transfer. *Management Science, 49*(4), 529–540.

5. Giacomantonio, M., Ten Velden, F. S., & De Dreu, C. K. (2016). Framing effortful strategies as easy enables depleted individuals to execute complex tasks effectively. *Journal of Experimental Social Psychology, 62*, 68–74.

6. According to the anchoring-information model (AIM), it is adviseable to make the first offer under conditions of information symmetry. Loschelder, D. D., Trotschel, R., Swaab, R. I., Friese, M., & Galinsky, A. D. (2016). The information-anchoring model of first offers: When moving first helps or hurts negotiators. *Journal of Applied Psychology, 101*(7), 995-1012).

7. Kray, L. J., Galinsky, A. D., & Thompson, L. (2002). Reversing the gender gap in negotiations: An exploration of stereotype regeneration. *Organizational Behavior and Human Decision Processes, 87*(2), 386–409.

8. Schank, R. C., Berman, T. R., Macpherson, K. A. (1999). Learning by doing, In Reigeluth, C. M. (Ed.), *Instructional-design theories and models: A new paradigm of instructional theory* (pp. 161–182). Lawrence Erlbaum Associates.

9. Wood, R., & Bandura, A. (1989). Impact of conceptions of ability on self-regulatory mechanisms and complex decision making. *Journal of Personality and Social Psychology, 56*(3), 407–415.

CHAPTER FIVE

1. Fry, W. R., Firestone, I. J., & Williams, D. L. (1983). Negotiation process and outcome of stranger dyads and dating cou-

ples: Do lovers lose? *Basic and Applied Social Psychology, 4*(1), 1–16.

2. The statistical results reported were of marginal significance.

3. Schoeninger, D. W., & Wood, W. D. (1969). Comparison of married and ad hoc mixed-sex dyads negotiating the division of a reward. *Journal of Experimental Social Psychology, 5*(4), 483–499.

4. Thompson, L., Peterson, E., & Brodt, S. E. (1996). Team negotiation: An examination of integrative and distributive bargaining. *Journal of Personality and Social Psychology, 70*(1), 66; Peterson, E., & Thompson, L. (1997). Negotiation teamwork: The impact of information distribution and accountability on performance depends on the relationship among team members. *Organizational Behavior and Human Decision Processes, 72*(3), 364–383.

5. Harvey, J. B. (1974). The Abilene paradox: The management of agreement. *Organizational Dynamics, 3*(1), 63–80.

6. Story based on Harvey, J. B. (1974). The Abilene paradox: The management of agreement. *Organizational Dynamics, 3*(1), 63–80.

7. Clark, M. S., Mills, J. R., & Corcoran, D. M. (1989). Keeping track of needs and inputs of friends and strangers. *Personality and Social Psychology Bulletin, 15*(4), 533–542.

8. Ross, M., & Sicoly, F. (1979). Egocentric biases in availability and attribution. *Journal of Personality and Social Psychology, 37*(3), 322.

9. Messick, D. M., & Sentis, K. P. (1979). Fairness and preference. *Journal of Experimental Social Psychology, 15*(4), 418–434.

10. Neves, P. (2012). Organizational cynicism: Spillover effects on supervisor–subordinate relationships and performance. *The Leadership Quarterly, 23*(5), 965–976.

11. Amanatullah, E. T., Morris, M. W., & Curhan, J. R. (2008). Negotiators who give too much: Unmitigated communion, relational anxieties, and economic costs in distributive and integrative bargaining. *Journal of Personality and Social Psychology, 95*(3), 723.

12. Amanatullah, E. T., Morris, M. W., & Curhan, J. R. (2008). Negotiators who give too much: Unmitigated communion,

relational anxieties, and economic costs in distributive and integrative bargaining. *Journal of Personality and Social Psychology, 95*(3), 723.

13. Curhan, J. R., Neale, M. A., Ross, L., & Rosencranz-Engelmann, J. (2008). Relational accommodation in negotiation: Effects of egalitarianism and gender on economic efficiency and relational capital. *Organizational Behavior and Human Decision Processes, 107*(2), 192–205.

14. Crotty, S., & Thompson, L. (2009). When your heart isn't smart: How different types of regret change decisions and profits. *International Journal of Conflict Management, 20*(4), 315–350.

15. Curhan, J. R., Neale, M. A., Ross, L., & Rosencranz-Engelmann, J. (2008). Relational accommodation in negotiation: Effects of egalitarianism and gender on economic efficiency and relational capital. *Organizational Behavior and Human Decision Processes, 107*(2), 192–205.

16. Henry, O. (1906). *The four million*. A. L. Burt Company.

17. Menon, T., & Thompson, L. (2007). Don't hate me because I'm beautiful: Self-enhancing biases in threat appraisal. *Organizational Behavior and Human Decision Processes, 104*(1), 45–60.

18. Kurtzberg, T. R., Naquin, C. E., & Belkin, L. Y. (2005). Electronic performance appraisals: The effects of e-mail communication on peer ratings in actual and simulated environments. *Organizational Behavior and Human Decision Processes, 98*(2), 216–226.

19. White, J. B., Tynan, R., Galinsky, A. D., & Thompson, L. (2004). Face threat sensitivity in negotiation: Roadblock to agreement and joint gain. *Organizational Behavior and Human Decision Processes, 94*(2), 102–124.

20. Savitsky, K., Keysar, B., Epley, N., Carter, T., & Swanson, A. (2011). The closeness-communication bias: Increased egocentrism among friends versus strangers. *Journal of Experimental Social Psychology, 47*(1), 269–273.

21. Savitsky, K., Keysar, B., Epley, N., Carter, T., & Swanson, A. (2011). The closeness-communication bias: Increased egocen-

trism among friends versus strangers. *Journal of Experimental Social Psychology, 47*(1), 269–273.

22. Savitsky, K., Keysar, B., Epley, N., Carter, T., & Swanson, A. (2011). The closeness-communication bias: Increased egocentrism among friends versus strangers. *Journal of Experimental Social Psychology, 47*(1), 269–273.

23. Stefanowitsch, A. (2003). A construction-based approach to indirect speech acts. *Pragmatics and Beyond New Series*, 105–126.

24. Bayat, N. (2013). A study on the use of speech acts. *Procedia-social and Behavioral Sciences, 70*, 213–221.

25. Overall, N. C., & McNulty, J. K. (2017). What type of communication during conflict is beneficial for intimate relationships? *Current Opinion in Psychology, 13*, 1–5.

26. Gilovich, T., Savitsky, K., Medvec, V. H. (1998). The illusion of transparency: Biased assessments of others' ability to read one's emotional states. *Journal of Personality and Social Psychology, 75*(2), 332–346.

27. Fleming, J. H., Darley, J. M., Hilton, J. L., & Kojetin, B. A. (1990). Multiple audience problem: A strategic communication perspective on social perception. *Journal of Personality and Social Psychology, 58*(4), 593.

28. Keysar, B., & Henly, A. S. (2002). Speakers' overestimation of their effectiveness. *Psychological Science, 13*(3), 207–212.

29. Rogers, C. (1980). *A Way of Being*. Houghton Mifflin Co.

30. Raab, D. (2017, February 6). 6 ways to nurture empathy in intimate relationships. *Psychology Today*. psychologytoday.com

31. Beckes, L., Coan, J. A., & Hasselmo, K. (2012). Familiarity promotes the blurring of self and other in the neural representation of threat. *Social Cognitive and Affective Neuroscience, 8*(6), 670–677.

32. Galinsky, A. D., Maddux, W. W., Gilin, D., & White, J. B. (2008). Why it pays to get inside the head of your opponent: The differential effects of perspective-taking and empathy in strategic interactions. *Psychological Science, 19*(4), 378–384.

33. Gillin, D., Maddux, W. W., Carpenter, J., & Galinsky, A. D. (2013). When to use your head and when to use your heart: The differential value of perspective-taking versus empathy in

competitive interactions. *Personality and Social Psychology Bulletin, 39*(1), 3–16.

34. Sinaceur, M. (2010). Suspending judgment to create value: Suspicion and trust in negotiation. *Journal of Experimental Social Psychology, 46*(3), 543–550.

35. Thomas, S. P., Groer, M., Davis, M., Droppleman, P., Mozingo, J., & Pierce, M. (2000). Anger and cancer: An analysis of the linkages. *Cancer Nursing, 23*(5), 344–349.

36. Firestone, R. (2014, October 28). The simple truth about anger. *Psychology Today*. psychologytoday.com

37. Goleman, D. (Ed.). (2003). *Healing emotions: Conversations with the Dalai Lama on mindfulness, emotions, and health*. Shambhala Publications.

38. Lindquist, K. A., Wager, T. D., Kober, H., Bliss-Moreau, E., & Barrett, L. F. (2012). The brain basis of emotion: A meta-analytic review. *The Behavioral and Brain Sciences, 35*(3), 121.8.

39. Van Kleef, G. A., De Dreu, C. K. W., & Manstead, A. S. R. (2006). Supplication and appeasement in conflict and negotiation: The interpersonal effects of disappointment, worry, guilt, and regret. *Journal of Personality and Social Psychology, 91*(1), 124–142.

40. Van Kleef, G. A., & Van Lange, P. A. M. (2008). What other's disappointment may do to selfish people: Emotion and social value orientation in a negotiation context. *Personality and Social Psychology Bulletin, 34*(8), 1084–1095.

41. Swaab, R. I., & Swaab, D. F. (2009, January). Sex differences in the effects of visual contact and eye contact in negotiations. *Journal of Experimental Social Psychology, 45*(1), 129–136.

42. Mehrabian, A., & Diamond, S. G. (1971). Seating arrangement and conversation. *Sociometry*, 281–289.

43. Zhu, R., & Argo, J. J. (2013). Exploring the impact of various shaped seating arrangements on persuasion. *Journal of Consumer Research, 40*(2), 336–349.

44. Kray, L. J., Galinsky, A. D., & Thompson, L. (2002). Reversing the gender gap in negotiations: An exploration of stereotype regeneration. *Organizational Behavior and Human Decision*

Processes, 87(2), 386–409; Kray, L. J., Thompson, L., & Galinsky, A. (2001). Battle of the sexes: Gender stereotype confirmation and reactance in negotiations. *Journal of Personality and Social Psychology, 80*(6), 942.

45. Ayres, I., & Siegelman, P. (1995). Race and gender discrimination in bargaining for a new car. *American Economic Review*, 304–321.

46. Ben-Yoav, O., & Pruitt, D. G. (1984). Accountability to constituents: A two-edged sword. *Organizational Behavior and Human Performance, 34*(3), 283–295.

47. Bowles, H. R., Babcock, L., & McGinn, K. L. (2005). Constraints and triggers: Situational mechanics of gender in negotiation. *Journal of Personality and Social Psychology, 89*(6), 951.

48. Curhan, J. (2019). Silence is golden: Silence, deliberative mindset and value creation in negotiation, working paper; Cho, Y., Zhang, T., Overbeck, J. R., Yang, Y., & Curhan, J. (2017). Quiet the mind or just be quiet: Consequences of silence in negotiation. In E. Hart and M. Schweitzer (chairs), Promoting cooperation in competitive negotiations: Which communication strategies help and hurt? Symposium conducted at the 77th Academy of Management Annual Meeting, Anaheim, California.

49. Clark, M. S., & Mills, J. (1979). Interpersonal attraction in exchange and communal relationships. *Journal of Personality and Social Psychology, 37*(1), 12–24.

50. Thompson, L. & DeHarpport, T. (1998). Relationships, goal incompatibility, and communal orientation in negotiations. *Basic and Applied Psychology, 20*(1), 33–44.

51. McGinn, K. L., & Keros, A. T. (2002). Improvisation and the logic of exchange in socially embedded transactions. *Administrative Science Quarterly, 47*(3), 442–473.

52. McGinn, K. L., & Keros, A. T. (2002). Improvisation and the logic of exchange in socially embedded transactions. *Administrative Science Quarterly, 47*(3), 442–473.

53. Tinsley, C. H., O'Connor, K. M., & Sullivan, B. A. (2002). Tough guys finish last: The perils of a distributive reputation. *Organizational Behavior and Human Decision Processes, 88*(2), 621–642.

54. Liberman, V., Samuels, S. M., & Ross, L. (2004). The name of the game: Predictive power of reputations versus situational labels in determining prisoner's dilemma game moves. *Personality and Social Psychology Bulletin, 30*(9), 1175–1185.

55. Menon, T., & Thompson, L. (2007). Don't hate me because I'm beautiful: Self-enhancing biases in threat appraisal. *Organizational Behavior and Human Decision Processes, 104*(1), 45–60.

56. Seider, B. H., Hirschberger, G., Nelson, K. L., & Levenson, R. W. (2009). We can work it out: Age differences in relational pronouns, physiology, and behavior in marital conflict. *Psychology and Aging, 24*(3), 604.

57. Maddux, W. W., Mullen, E., & Galinsky, A. D. (2008, March). Chameleons bake bigger pies and take bigger pieces: Strategic behavior mimicry facilitates negotiation outcomes. *Journal of Experimental Social Psychology, 44*(2), 461–468.

58. Festinger, L. (1962). *A theory of cognitive dissonance* (Vol. 2). Stanford University Press.

CHAPTER SIX

1. Sandberg, S. (2013). *Lean in: Women, work, and the will to lead*. Knopf.

2. *Should Women "Lean In" to Create More Value in Negotiations?* (2018, October 30). Program on Negotiation. www.pon.harvard.edu

3. Morgenstern, O., & Von Neumann, J. (1953). *Theory of games and economic behavior*. Princeton University Press.

4. Bohn, H. G. (1851.) *New handbook of games*. Henry F. Anners.

5. Thompson, L. L. (1991). Information exchange in negotiation. *Journal of Experimental Social Psychology, 27*(2), 161–179.

6. Elkins, K. (2017, May 11). Lady Gaga's former manager shares the key to getting what you want in a negotiation. *CNBC*. cnbc.com; Sacks, D. (2014, January 13). Troy Carter: Fired by Lady Gaga and loving it. *Fast Company*. fastcompany.com

7. Patterson, T. (2016, April 28). Delta buys 75 new Bombardier jets. *CNN Money*. money.cnn.com

8. Kwak, S. (2013, January 6). Who gets what: Key points of the NHL's new CBA deal. *Sports Illustrated*. sportsillustrated.cnn .com

9. Raiffa, H. (1982). *The art and science of negotiation*. Belknap.

10. Rousseau, D. (1995). *Psychological contracts in organizations: Understanding written and unwritten agreements*. Sage Publications; Rousseau, D. M. (1998). The 'problem' of the psychological contract considered. *Journal of Organizational Behavior: The International Journal of Industrial, Occupational and Organizational Psychology and Behavior, 19*(S1), 665–671; Rousseau, D. M., & Tijoriwala, S. A. (1998). Assessing psychological contracts: Issues, alternatives and measures. *Journal of Organizational Behavior: The International Journal of Industrial, Occupational and Organizational Psychology and Behavior, 19*(S1), 679–695.

11. Carr, A. (2013, July). The hard sell at Taco Bell. *Fast Company*. fastcompany.com; Lutz, A. (2014, February 26). How Taco Bell's lead innovator created the most successful menu item of all time. *Business Insider*. businessinsider.com

12. Carr, A. (2013, July). The hard sell at Taco Bell. *Fast Company*. fastcompany.com; Lutz, A. (2014, February 26). How Taco Bell's lead innovator created the most successful menu item of all time. *Business Insider*. businessinsider.com

13. Littleton, C. (2017, December 14). Disney-Fox deal: How secret, "smooth and cordial" negotiations drove a blockbuster acquisition. *Variety*. variety.com

14. James, M. (2019, March 19). Disney-Fox deal is complete; CEO Bob Iger's big swing could change media industry, *LA Times*. latimes.com

15. Susskind, L. E., & Rumore, D. (2015). Using devising seminars to advance collaborative problem solving in complicated public policy disputes. *Negotiation Journal, 31*(3), 223–235.

16. Robinson, R. J., & Keltner, D. (1996). Much ado about nothing? Revisionists and traditionalists choose an introductory

English syllabus. *Psychological Science, 7*(1), 18–24; Ross, L., & Stillinger, C. (1991). Barriers to conflict resolution. *Negotiation Journal, 7*(4), 389–404; Stillinger, C. A. (1988). *The reactive devaluation barrier to conflict resolution* (No. 3). Stanford Center on Conflict and Negotiation, Stanford University.

17. Ross, L., & Stillinger, C. A. (1988). *Psychological barriers to conflict resolution* (No. 4). Stanford Center on Conflict and Negotiation, Stanford University.

18. Oskamp, S., & Hartry, A. (1968). A factor-analytic study of the double standard in attitudes toward US and Russian actions. *Behavioral Science, 13*(3), 178–188.

19. Gillespie, J. J., & Bazerman, M. H. (1998). Pre-settlement settlement (PreSS): A simple technique for initiating complex negotiations. *Negotiation Journal, 14*(2), 149–159.

20. De Dreu, C. K. W., Giacomantonio, M., Shalvi, S., & Sligte, D. (2009). Getting stuck or stepping back: Effects of obstacles and construal level in the negotiation of creative solutions. *Journal of Experimental Social Psychology, 45*(3), 542–548.

21. Eyal, T., Sagristano, M. D., Trope, Y., Liberman, N., & Chaiken, S. (2009). When values matter: Expressing values in behavioral intentions for the near vs. distant future. *Journal of Experimental Social Psychology, 45*(1), 35–43.

22. Henderson, M. D. (2011). Mere physical distance and integrative agreements: When more space improves negotiation outcomes. *Journal of Experimental Social Psychology, 47*(1), 7–15.

23. Giacomantonio, M., De Dreu, C. K., & Mannetti, L. (2010). Now you see it, now you don't: Interests, issues, and psychological distance in integrative negotiation. *Journal of Personality and Social Psychology, 98*(5), 761.

24. Mannix, E. A., Tinsley, C. H., & Bazerman, M. (1995). Negotiating over time: Impediments to integrative solutions. *Organizational Behavior and Human Decision Processes, 62*(3), 241–251.

25. Schroeder, J., Risen, J. L., Gino, F., & Norton, M. I. (2019). Handshaking promotes deal-making by signaling cooperative intent. *Journal of Personality and Social Psychology, 116*(5), 743.

26. De Dreu, C. K. (2012). Oxytocin modulates cooperation within and competition between groups: An integrative review and research agenda. *Hormones and Behavior, 61*(3), 419–428.

27. De Dreu, C. K., Shalvi, S., Greer, L. L., Van Kleef, G. A., & Handgraaf, M. J. (2012). Oxytocin motivates non-cooperation in intergroup conflict to protect vulnerable in-group members. *PloS one, 7*(11), e46751.

CHAPTER SEVEN

1. Bailenson, J. (2020, April 3). Why Zoom meetings can exhaust us. *Wall Street Journal.* wsj.com

2. Noah, S. (2012, Wednesday, July 18). Texting overtakes talking as most popular form of communication in UK. *Independent.* independent.co.uk

3. Burke, K. (2018, May 18). How many texts do people send every day (2018)? *Text Requests.* textrequest.com

4. Millennials shun face-to-face conversations for online chats. (2018, January 29). *Cancer Research UK.* cancerresearchuk.org

5. Turkle, S. (2012, April 21). The flight from conversation. *New York Times.* nytimes.com

6. Schade, L. C., Sandberg, J., Bean, R., Busby, D., & Coyne, S. (2013). Using technology to connect in romantic relationships: Effects on attachment, relationship satisfaction, and stability in emerging adults. *Journal of Couple and Relationship Therapy, 12*, 314–338.

7. Foster, B. L. (2016, October 28). Married to their smartphones (oh, and to each other, too). *New York Times.* nytimes.com

8. Fratti, K. (2017, September 15). 6 texting habits couples in the strongest relationships have. *Hello Giggles.* hellogiggles.com

9. Dettmers, J., Vahle-Hinz, T., Bamberg, E., Friedrich, N., & Keller, M. (2016). Extended work availability and its relation with start-of-day mood and cortisol. *Journal of Occupational Health Psychology, 21*(1), 105.

10. Becker, W. J., Belkin, L., & Tuskey, S. (2018, July). Killing me softly: Electronic communications monitoring and employee and spouse well-being. In *Academy of Management Proceedings* (Vol. 2018, No. 1, p. 12574). Academy of Management.

11. Becker, W. J., Belkin, L., & Tuskey, S. (2018, July). Killing me softly: Electronic communications monitoring and employee and spouse well-being. In *Academy of Management Proceedings* (Vol. 2018, No. 1, p. 12574). Academy of Management.

12. Ross, D. S., & Vasantha, S. (2014). A conceptual study on impact of stress on work-life balance. *Sai Om Journal of Commerce & Management, 1*(2), 61–65; Becker, W. J., Belkin, L., & Tuskey, S. (2018, July). Killing me softly: Electronic communications monitoring and employee and spouse well-being. In *Academy of Management Proceedings* (Vol. 2018, No. 1, p. 12574). Academy of Management.

13. Jane, T. (2018, January 20). Complaining about low pay online "destroyed my life." *New York Post.* nypost.com

14. Premiere Global Services. (2019). *Evolution of Sales: The Survival Guide*. [PDF file]. business.linkedin.com/content/dam/business/sales-solutions/global/en_US/c/pdfs/pgi-ebook-the-evolution-of-sales-the-survival-guide-en-us.pdf

15. Premiere Global Services. (2019). Evolution of Sales: The Survival Guide. [PDF file]. business.linkedin.com/content/dam/business/sales-solutions/global/en_US/c/pdfs/pgi-ebook-the-evolution-of-sales-the-survival-guide-en-us.pdf

16. Ellis, A., & Beattie, G. (1986). Language reception: Recognizing spoken and written words. *The Psychology of Language and Communication*, 211–227.

17. Newman, S. A., Ford, R. C., & Marshall, G. W. (2019). Virtual team leader communication: Employee perception and organizational reality. *International Journal of Business Communication*, DOI:2329488419829895.

18. Schrage, M. (1995, November 26). New technologies are forcing workers to act more human. *Los Angeles Times.* latimes.com

19. Dubrovsky, V. J., Kiesler, S., & Sethna, B. N. (1991). The equalization phenomenon: Status effects in computer-mediated

and face-to-face decision-making groups. *Human-Computer Interaction, 6*(2), 119–146.

20. Comstock, C. (2010). Read the letter an employee sent to HR complaining about his boss' bullying. *Business Insider*. businessinsider.com

21. Murphy, S. (2008, November 6). How I avoid sending email I regret. *SKMurphy*. skmurphy.com

22. Green, A. (2019, January 29). My boss accidentally sent me a message complaining about me. *Ask a Manager*. askamanager.org

23. Kellermann, K. (1984). The negativity effect and its implications for initial interaction. *Communication Monographs, 51*(1), 37–55.

24. Kurtzberg, T. R., Naquin, C. E., & Belkin, L. Y. (2005). Electronic performance appraisals: The effects of e-mail communication on peer ratings in actual and simulated environments. *Organizational Behavior and Human Decision Processes, 98*(2), 216–226.

25. Roghanizad, M. M., & Bohns, V. K. (2017). Ask in person: You're less persuasive than you think over email. *Journal of Experimental Social Psychology, 69*, 223–226.

26. 16 secrets of engaging remote meetings. (2019, September 30). *MiroBlog*. miro.com/blog

27. Morris, M., Nadler, J., Kurtzberg, T., & Thompson, L. (2002). Schmooze or lose: Social friction and lubrication in e-mail negotiations. *Group Dynamics: Theory, Research, and Practice, 6*(1), 89–100.

28. Farrell, J., and Rabin, M. (1996). Cheap Talk. *Journal of Economic Perspectives, 10*(3), 103–118.

29. Valley, K., Thompson, L., Gibbons, R., & Bazerman, M. H. (2002). How communication improves efficiency in bargaining games. *Games and Economic Behavior, 38*(1), 127–155.

30. Ireland, M. E., & Henderson, M. D. (2014). Language style matching, engagement, and impasse in negotiations. *Negotiation and Conflict Management Research, 7*(1), 1–16.

31. Collot, M., & Belmore, N. (1996). A new variety of English. *Computer-mediated communication: Linguistic, social, and cross-cultural perspectives, 39*, 13.

32. Lincke, A., & Ulijn, J. (2004). The effect of CMC and FTF on negotiation outcomes between R&D and manufacturing part-

ners in the supply chain: An Anglo/Nordic/Latin comparison. *International Negotiation, 9*(1), 111–140.

33. Bryant, A. (2015, October 17). Lars Dalgaard: Build trust by daring to show that you're human. *New York Times.* nytimes .com

34. Berry, T. (2018, December 21). 10 new rules for business emails. *Small Business Trends.* smallbiztrends.com

35. Niederhoffer, K. G., & Pennebaker, J. W. (2002). Linguistic style matching in social interaction. *Journal of Language and Social Psychology, 21*(4), 337–360; Niederhoffer, K. G., & Pennebaker, J. W. (2002). Sharing one's story: On the benefits of writing or talking about emotional experience. In C. R. Snyder & S. J. Lopez (Eds.), *Handbook of positive psychology* (pp. 573–583). New York: Oxford University Press; Taylor, P. J. (2002). A cylindrical model of communication behavior in crisis negotiations. *Human Communication Research, 28*(1), 7–48.

36. Niederhoffer, K. G., & Pennebaker, J. W. (2002). Linguistic style matching in social interaction. *Journal of Language and Social Psychology, 21*(4), 337–360.

37. Ireland, M. E., Slatcher, R. B., Eastwick, P. W., Scissors, L. E., Finkel, E. J., & Pennebaker, J. W. (2011). Language style matching predicts relationship initiation and stability. *Psychological Science, 22*(1), 39–44; Ireland, M. E., & Henderson, M. D. (2014). Language style matching, engagement, and impasse in negotiations. *Negotiation and Conflict Management Research, 7*(1): 1-16; Niederhoffer, K. G., & Pennebaker, J. W. (2002). Linguistic style matching in social interaction. *Journal of Language and Social Psychology, 21*(4), 337–360.

38. Niederhoffer, K. G., & Pennebaker, J. W. (2002). Linguistic style matching in social interaction. *Journal of Language and Social Psychology, 21*(4), 337–360; Niederhoffer, K. G., & Pennebaker, J. W. (2002). Sharing one's story: On the benefits of writing or talking about emotional experience. In C. R. Snyder & S. J. Lopez (Eds.), *Handbook of positive psychology* (pp. 573–583). Oxford University Press.

39. Bayram, A. B., & Ta, V. P. (2019). Diplomatic chameleons: Language style matching and agreement in international dip-

lomatic negotiations. *Negotiation and Conflict Management Research, 12*(1), 23–40.

40. Bowen, J. D., Winczewski, L. A., & Collins, N. L. (2017). Language style matching in romantic partners' conflict and support interactions. *Journal of Language and Social Psychology, 36(*3), 263–286.

41. Ireland, M. E., & Henderson, M. D. (2014). Language style matching, engagement, and impasse in negotiations. *Negotiation and Conflict Management Research, 7*(1), 1–16.

42. Donohue, W. A., & Liang, Y. J. (2011). Transformative linguistic styles in divorce mediation. *Negotiation and Conflict Management Research, 4*(3), 200–218.

43. Niederhoffer, K. G., & Pennebaker, J. W. (2002). Linguistic style matching in social interaction. *Journal of Language and Social Psychology, 21*(4), 337–360; Taylor, P. J. (2002). A cylindrical model of communication behavior in crisis negotiations. *Human Communication Research, 28*(1), 7–48.

44. Bell, A., Brenier, J. M., Gregory, M. G., Girand, C., and Jurafsky, D. (2009, January). Predictability effects on durations of content and function words in conversational English. *Journal of Memory and Language, 60*(1), 92–111.

45. Ireland, M. E., & Pennebaker, J. W. (2010). Language style matching in writing: Synchrony in essays, correspondence, and poetry. *Journal of Personality and Social Psychology, 99*(3), 549–571; Tausczik, Y. R. (2012). *Changing group dynamics through computerized language feedback* (Doctoral dissertation).

46. Ireland, M. E. (2011). *Three explanations for the link between language style matching and liking* (Doctoral dissertation).

47. Taylor, P. J., & Thomas, S. (2008, August). Linguistic style matching and negotiation outcome. *Negotiation and Conflict Management Research, 1*(3), 263–281.

48. Giles, H., & Coupland, N. (1991). *Mapping social psychology. Language: Contexts and consequences.* Thomson Brooks/Cole Publishing Co.; Giles, H. (2016). Communication accommodation theory. *The International Encyclopedia of Communication Theory and Philosophy*, 1–7.

49. Moore, D. A., Kurtzberg, T. R., Thompson, L., & Morris, M. W. (1999). Long and short routes to success in electronically-mediated

negotiations: Group affiliations and good vibrations. *Organizational Behavior and Human Decision Processes, 77*, 22–43.

50. Heine, S. J., Takemoto, T., Moskalenko, S., Lasaleta, J., & Henrich, J. (2008). Mirrors in the head: Cultural variation in objective self-awareness. *Personality and Social Psychology Bulletin, 34*(7), 879–887.

51. Thompson, L. L. (1991). Information exchange in negotiation. *Journal of Experimental Social Psychology, 27*(2), 161–179.

52. Kramer, R. M. (1995). Power, paranoia, and distrust in organizations: The distorted view from the top. *Research on Negotiation in Organizations, 5*, 119–154.

53. Keltner, D., Gruenfeld, D. H., Anderson, C. (2003, April). Power, approach, and inhibition. *Psychological Review, 110*(2), 265–284.

54. dos Santos, V. P. (2002). Genre analysis of business letters of negotiation. *English for Specific Purposes, 21*(2), 167–199.

55. Volkema, R. J., Fleck, D., & Hofmeister, A. (2011). Getting off on the right foot: The effects of initial email messages on negotiation process and outcome. *IEEE Transactions on Professional Communication, 54*(3), 299–313.

56. Owen, M. (1983). *Apologies and remedial interchanges: A study of language use in social interaction*. Mouton de Gruyter.

57. Brooks, A. W., Dai, H., & Schweitzer, M. E. (2014). I'm sorry about the rain! Superfluous apologies demonstrate empathic concern and increase trust. *Social Psychological and Personality Science, 5*(4), 467–474.

58. Harrison, S., & Allton, D. (2013). Apologies in email discussions. In Herring, S., Stein, D., & Virtanen, T. (Eds.). (2013). *Pragmatics of computer-mediated communication* (pp. 315–338). Boston, MA: Walter de Gruyter.

59. Steinberg, S. (2019, August 28). The best way to apologize when you've screwed up at work. *Quartz at Work.* qz.com

60. Martinovski, B., Traum, D., & Marsella, S. (2007, January). Rejection of empathy in negotiation. *Group Decision and Negotiation, 16*(1), 61–76.

61. Zhou, L., Sung, Y-W., & Zhang, D. (2013). Deception performance in online group negotiation and decision making: The

effects of deception experience and deception skill. *Group Decision and Negotiation, 22*(1), 153–172.

62. Hancock, J. T., Thom-Santelli, J., & Ritchie, T. (2004, April). Deception and design: The impact of communication technology on lying behavior. *In Proceedings of the SIGCHI conference on human factors in computing systems* (pp. 129–134). ACM.

63. O'Sullivan, M., Frank, M. G., Hurley, C. M., & Tiwana, J. (2009). Police lie detection accuracy: The effect of lie scenario. *Law and Human Behavior, 33*(6), 530.

64. Ekman, P. (2009). *Telling lies: Clues to deceit in the marketplace, politics, and marriage* (revised edition). W. W. Norton & Company.

65. Hancock, J. T., Curry, L. E., Goorha, S., & Woodworth, M. (2007). On lying and being lied to: A linguistic analysis of deception in computer-mediated communication. *Discourse Processes, 45*(1), 1–23.

66. Keila, P. S., & Skillicorn, D. B. (2005, June). Detecting unusual and deceptive communication in email. In Centers for Advanced Studies Conference (pp. 17–20).

67. Ambady, N., & Rosenthal, R. (1992). Thin slices of expressive behavior as predictors of interpersonal consequences: A meta-analysis. *Psychological Bulletin, 111*(2), 256; Borkenau, P., Mauer, N., Riemann, R., Spinath, F. M., & Angleitner, A. (2004). Thin slices of behavior as cues of personality and intelligence. *Journal of Personality and Social Psychology, 86*(4), 599–614.

68. Brennan, N., & Conroy, J. (2013). Executive hubris: The case of a bank CEO. *Accounting, Auditing & Accountability Journal, 26*(2), 172–195.

69. Owen, D., & Davidson, J. (2009). Hubris syndrome: An acquired personality disorder? A study of US Presidents and UK Prime Ministers over the last 100 years. *Brain, 132*(5), 1396–1406.

CHAPTER EIGHT

1. Lally, P., Van Jaarsveld, C. H., Potts, H. W., & Wardle, J. (2010). How are habits formed: Modelling habit formation in

the real world. *European Journal of Social Psychology, 40*(6), 998–1009.

2. Gentner, D., Loewenstein, J., & Thompson, L. (2003). Learning and transfer: A general role for analogical encoding. *Journal of Educational Psychology, 95*(2), 393.

3. Renkl, A., Mandl, H., & Gruber, H. (1996). Inert knowledge: Analyses and remedies. *Educational Psychologist, 31*(2), 115-121.

4. Kim, J., Thompson, L., & Loewenstein, J. (2019). Open for learning: Encouraging generalization fosters knowledge transfer in negotiation. *Negotiation and Conflict Management Research, 13*(1), 3-23.

Index

communal orientation, 81
communal relationships,
   transactional vs., 44
communication
  direct, 56
  etiquette for virtual, 143,
    164–66, *see also* emails
  indirect, 53–60
  types of, 145–46
Communication
  Accommodation Theory,
  171
competitive personality types, 5
construal theory, 135
continued training, 197–98
convergence, 171
cooperative personality types, 5
cortisol, 143–44
couples, negotiations in, 39–40
couple social science research,
  39–40
Crotty, Susan, 49
Crowe, Russell, 15
culture, egalitarian, 50–51
Curhan, Jared, 6–7, 49–50, 78

Dalai Lama, 68
Dalgaard, Lars, 164–65
dance of communication, 146
deals, interim, 132–33
Dean, John, 167
deception, 183–85
Delta Air Lines, 111
"dessert tray" method, 112–14
devalue-the-author effect, 129
devising seminars, 126
didactic learning, 30–31

direct communication, 56
disappointment hack, 69
Disney, 123–24
distrust, suspicion vs., 66–67
DLT (Doritos Locos Taco), 123
"don't-rock-the-boat" trap, 44
Doritos Locos Taco (DLT), 123
Dr. Jekyll and Mr. Hyde effect,
  147–50
Dual-Concern model, 4
Duffield, John, 149

"easy-to-use" tactics, 31–32
Eat24, 144
E-charisma, 152–55
e-communication. *see* virtual
  life negotiations
egalitarian culture, 50–51
egocentric bias effect, 45–46
Ekman, Paul, 184
elevator pitch, 194–95
emails
  and cortisol, 143–44
  etiquette for, 149, 164–66
  and power differentials,
   179–80
  and unintended email
   recipients, 150
  see also virtual life
   negotiations
emotional punctuation, 83
empathy, 61–65
Enron, 185
etiquette, communication, 143,
  164–66
Even-Steven trap, 8–10
Evershed, Patrick, 149

About the Author

LEIGH THOMPSON is the J. Jay Gerber Distinguished Professor of Dispute Resolution and Organizations at the Kellogg School of Management, Northwestern University. An acclaimed researcher, author, and speaker, Thompson has developed several online courses on negotiation, leading teams, creativity, and virtual collaboration. Thompson's books include *Creative Conspiracy: The New Rules of Breakthrough Collaboration*, *Making the Team*, *The Mind and Heart of the Negotiator*, *The Truth About Negotiations*, and *Stop Spending, Start Managing*.